THE GRIT AND THE COURAGE

Stories of Success in an Unforgiving Land

THE GRIT AND THE COURAGE

Stories of Success in an Unforgiving Land

STEVE BARTLETT

St. John's, Newfoundland and Labrador
2008

© 2008, Steve Bartlett

 Canada Council Conseil des Arts
for the Arts du Canada

Canadä

 Newfoundland
Labrador

We gratefully acknowledge the financial support of the Canada Council for the Arts, the
Government of Canada through the Book Publishing Industry Development Program
(BPIDP), and the Government of Newfoundland and Labrador through the Department of
Tourism, Culture and Recreation for our publishing program.

Cover design by Todd Manning
Layout by Joanne Snook-Hann
Printed on acid-free paper

Published by
CREATIVE PUBLISHERS
an imprint of CREATIVE BOOK PUBLISHING
a Transcontinental Inc. associated company
P.O. Box 8660, Stn. A
St. John's, Newfoundland and Labrador A1B 3T7

Printed in Canada by:
TRANSCONTINENTAL INC.

Library and Archives Canada Cataloguing in Publication

Bartlett, Steve, 1968-
    The grit and the courage : stories of success in an unforgiving land / Steve
Bartlett.

"Vol. 1".
ISBN 978-1-897174-29-6 (v. 1)

1. Success in business--Newfoundland and Labrador. 2. Business enterprises--
Newfoundland and Labrador. 3. Businesspeople--Newfoundland and Labrador--
Biography. I. Title.

HC112.5.A2B37 2008   338.092'2718   C2008-901893-1

For my dad, Gord Bartlett

INTRODUCTION

From Alex to Zita

Like anyone else, acquaintances and friends ask me what I'm doing when we meet through work, while picking up groceries or during a beer run. These past few months my answer has been different than usual. I was writing a book, and telling people that often made me feel somewhat shy and completely awkward.

"Oh," they would say, "what's the topic?"

After replying that it was successful Newfoundlanders and Labradorians, there frequently came a common, but perhaps sad, reply.

"Are there any?" many would ask with a laugh.

It was funny the first few times, but after a while, I got tired of it. Yes, they were trying to be engaging and humourous, but, to me, the question said a little bit about our mindset. Even though Newfoundlanders and Labradorians are fiercely proud of where they are from and of their brethren who succeed, we sometimes fail to realize just how many people from these parts have achieved remarkable things. In fact, for a place with just over a half-million people – a small city, really – we have enjoyed a lot more success than people tend to think. Or at least that's my take it on it.

Now just because the words "success" and "succeed" have been used already, this is not a new age positive-thinking book like *The Secret*. It's not the stuff of motivational guru Anthony Robbins either. This book doesn't belong in the positive thinking and self-help section, although if someone is inspired by Alex Faulkner, Myra Bennett or Tommy Sexton, that's fantastic. And even though Craig Dobbin, W.J. Herder and Zita Cobb are featured, it is also not for the business shelves. There's no in-depth study of commerce or ideas on "How to get rich quick" here, although if you are moved and make millions by reading it, feel free to mail me a share of the wealth via the publisher.

That's what this book is not. What it is though, is an attempt to tell some of the remarkable stories of people who were born or drawn to this land and prospered in their own way. You see, I'm a writer, not a psychologist or business person. I'm hardly one to offer advice on overcoming adversity or tips on how to stay within a budget. However, I am keen on telling tales, especially about Newfoundlanders who've beaten the odds. It's always fascinated me how some people manage to not only eke out a living in a land too tough for the Vikings, but to reach heights many of us wouldn't dream about for fear of failure.

I've tried to represent a good cross-section of individuals who, through hard work, determination and believing in themselves, have done particularly well. The stories are about people who've achieved in a variety of different fields, including hockey, television, nursing and business. I selected these people because I felt they had terrific tales to tell. Alex Faulkner reached the National Hockey League at a time when a Newfoundlander had just as good of a chance of being the first person on the moon. After buying a single helicopter to help him access salmon pools, Craig Dobbin overcame numerous near misses and assembled the world's largest helicopter services company. Myra Bennett faced daunting challenges while nursing in northern Newfoundland during the 1920s and '30s, but instead of packing it in and applying her skills in less harsh lands, the English nurse stayed, rolling with the punches and providing selfless service to a people that needed her. Tommy Sexton dropped out of school, determined to be an actor. He not only achieved that goal, he helped create some of the funniest sketches and characters in the history of Canadian television. He also became a pioneer in gay rights and AIDS awareness. W.J. Herder started a daily newspaper in the face of skepticism. Almost 130 years later, his publication is alive and well, and very much a part of Newfoundland's history and social fabric. Zita Cobb went from growing up with no electricity to helping negotiate massive technology deals. She became one of the wealthiest people in Canada.

Compiling the material for these mini-biographies involved a mix of interviews and research. As I gathered facts and put the stories together, some common denominators surfaced. While the individuals in this book are quite different from each other, they were each committed, courageous, and determined in their own right. To achieve, they all dealt with doubts, fought fears and overcame obstacles.

After writing this book – my first – I can relate to some of that. Any time I got bogged down in the process, I'd look to the person being written about and realize that succeeding at anything involves – pardon the colloquial phrase – "sucking it up" and going for it. Here's hoping you learn half as much from these individuals as I did.

Steve Bartlett, October 2008

TABLE OF CONTENTS

ALEX FAULKNER

ALEX FAULKNER WAS too nervous to keep down the soft-boiled eggs he ordered in the dining room of the hotel. He was on an unexpected, whirlwind ride and nearly in a state of shock. Three nights ago, on Saturday, he had been in Harbour Grace, Newfoundland, practising at the S.W. Moores Arena with a young, but dominant, senior hockey team called the CeeBees. Now it was Tuesday and he was in Toronto, centre of the hockey universe.

The day before, he had skated with a major junior team called the Toronto Marlboros and he was now about to practise with the storied National Hockey League franchise he grew up idolizing during cold and snowy winters in Bishop's Falls, Newfoundland – the Toronto Maple Leafs.

On that November morning, the anxious Faulkner urged constantly during the ten minute walk from the hotel to Maple Leaf Gardens. He walked through the big doors with his skates in hand

and asked a security guy for directions to Mr. Imlach's office. The guard asked for Faulkner's name. Oddly enough, it turned out he was a Faulkner too. The twenty-four-year-old felt a sudden sense of security and found himself more at ease than minutes before.

Faulkner met with George "Punch" Imlach, the Maple Leafs' coach and general manager, and then went to the team's dressing room to get ready for that morning's practice.

A host of future hockey hall of famers greeted him. Johnny Bower. Frank Mahavolich. George Armstrong. Dave Keon. Bert Olmstead. Tim Horton. Allan Stanley. Red Kelly. It was one of the greatest rosters the Maple Leafs had ever assembled, and that Monday morning, those marquee players, as well as a supporting cast that included the likes of Eddy "The Entertainer" Shack, welcomed a smiling East Coaster with a buzz cut into the fold.

The Faulkners and their friends would play hockey immediately after school every day, regardless of frozen fingers and frostbitten feet, high winds and winter storms.

Even though he was just there to see what he could do, the players didn't come across as big and powerful, as might be expected. Instead, they made Faulkner – all 5'8" and 165 pounds of him – feel at home.

He found a spot in the dressing room, which was bigger than those back home, but not elaborate like ones equipped with hot tubs and weightrooms that today's pro hockey players enjoy. Faulkner put on the equipment supplied by the Leafs, and tried to focus on making the most out of the opportunity before him.

As a kid, he had envisioned playing with, and against, pros but had never imagined that it would actually happen. Pro hockey just wasn't an option for Newfoundland hockey players. Scouts paid no attention to the island. Its population was sparse and scattered. Its hockey program was primitive and, compared to the systems in provinces like Ontario and Quebec, unorganized.

Regardless, after being spotted during an exhibition game in St. John's by Toronto's assistant general manager King Clancy, the

Alex as a puck-chasing youngster in Bishop's Falls. Pictured in front are Alex and his brothers George and Lindy. In back are Wally Purchase, Tony Earle and Ray Boyd.

twenty-four-year-old Faulkner was in T.O. embarking on an unexpected chapter of a hockey career that had started on the frozen Exploits River many years before.

With no rink in Bishop's Falls, he had learned to skate as a young gaffer of four or five on a frozen pool of a roaring river known for breeding huge Atlantic salmon, not professional hockey players. Before he could skate, Faulkner would stand on his blades and the wind would blow him downstream.

Almost immediately after young Alex had stepped on the ice, his father Lester – a locomotive engineer – put a hockey stick in his hand. The more the boy grasped the straight-blade stick, the more he was gripped by the game.

Over the years, his four brothers came down with hockey fever too. There was always three Faulkers old enough to play together. As an older one grew out of the games, or graduated to a higher level of hockey, a younger one was there to follow.

In the late fall, before the Exploits iced over, they would tempt fate and play on frozen ponds. Once winter arrived and the pools of the river became rock solid, they would spend hours and hours chasing a puck.

The Faulkners and their friends would play hockey immediately after school every day, regardless of frozen fingers and frostbitten feet, high winds and winter storms. Games went on forever. Scores were kept until the boys simply lost track.

On Saturdays, they would spend the entire day on the river. They wouldn't even break to eat, and the Faulkner boys would go home at night to find a huge pot of something on the stove prepared by their mother Olive. If they wanted three plates of supper, the hockey-hungry boys had it. And each night, as soon as they had cleaned their supper plates, the Faulkners and their friends would head back down to the Exploits, in the feel-it-when-you-breathe coolness, to flood their rink with water they'd fetch by dipping empty salt-beef buckets into a hole cut through the ice.

Lester Faulkner encouraged the boys' love of hockey. A great influence on his sons, he was interested in keeping them occupied and out of trouble. He always made sure they were outfitted for hockey and soccer, a sport he had excelled at himself.

Incidentally, the Faulkners and their friends approached soccer in the summer in the same way they did hockey in the winter. They always had a soccer ball to kick around and would make their own playing field. First they'd cut posts and fence the area off. Then they would cut the grass. The fields were somewhat primitive but highly playable.

When Alex and his older brother George were teenagers, they took their hockey on the road – to nearby Botwood, a town with an indoor, natural ice rink at the time. They would pile in the back of a truck and go there to play pick-up hockey, scrap games with no schedules or age limits.

Whoever played, played.

Around the same time, Faulkner started playing with the team from his school, Bishop's Falls Amalgamated. The opponents were Grand Falls Academy and Notre Dame Academy. The hockey was fairly organized, but nothing at all like the minor programs most kids today take for granted.

Faulkner began playing "official" hockey at the age of sixteen, after he was approached to join a junior all-star team in Grand Falls, a town roughly nine miles away from Bishop's Falls. That squad was called the Junior Ancos and its schedule in Faulkner's first year was almost as short as a hockey team's could be. It would play in an all-Newfoundland tourney against a single opponent, Buchans, in a best two-out-of-three series.

The fiery Faulkner didn't know what to expect and he didn't give it much thought either. As he did whenever he put on his gear – whether on the Exploits or at Botwood – he just went out and gave it everything he had.

That approach made him a stand-out for the Junior Ancos in the matchups against Buchans. In the series opener, Faulkner scored fast and often – four times in just twenty-eight seconds. He went on to make the goal light flash six more times in the two games, leading the team to the championship and earning himself the award as the tournament's most valuable player.

A year later, he climbed the hockey ranks to Grand

Alex in 1952 as a 16-year-old standout with the Grand Falls Junior Ancos.

Falls' senior B team. And the season that followed that, at eighteen, he led Grand Falls' senior A team to the Herder Memorial Trophy, Newfoundland's version of the Stanley Cup. He was named the most valuable player of the Herder playoffs.

With Faulkner playing a key role, the team hoisted the Herder three additional times after that.

It was around this time when he got an indication that he might have the potential to play beyond the shores of his island home. In

The five Faulkner brothers and their father in 1956. Pictured left to right are Alex, Lindy, George, Lester, Seth and Jack. The photo was taken at a game against a group of NHL players who toured Newfoundland.

the early '50s, the Boston Bruins visited Grand Falls and the five Faulkner brothers each played a couple of shifts against the National Hockey League team.

During one face-off, a Bruins player named Cal Gardner asked Faulkner if he had ever thought about going to the Mainland to play hockey. Flattered and shocked, Faulkner simply told Gardner that he had no plans to go away. It was something Newfoundland players didn't ordinarily do or plan.

Still, his older brother George had been giving it a shot. The second oldest Faulkner boy – Lindy was the oldest and Alex was the third-born – had left Bishop's Falls in the early '50s to play junior hockey in Quebec. After two seasons, George had graduated to the Quebec Hockey League and the Shawinigan Falls Cataracts.

He came within a skate edge of playing in the National Hockey League with the Montreal Canadiens.

George enjoyed four successful seasons with Shawinigan-Falls, but was simply unable to crack the legendary line-up being iced by the Habs at the time. Among the players wearing the bleu, blanc et rouge were Maurice "Rocket" Richard, Jean Beliveau, Bernie "Boom-Boom" Geoffrion, Dickie Moore, and Henri "The Pocket Rocket" Richard.

It was George's return to Newfoundland after the realization that he would never don a Canadiens' jersey that ended up opening the dressing room door for his brother Alex to get his shot. George came back after the 1958 season and started searching for a job. For a time, he and his wife stayed with a friend in Brigus, a small community in Conception Bay. Their host suggested that George look for work in nearby Harbour Grace, where a new stadium had just been built. He took the advice and ended up meeting with Lorne Wakelin, the stadium manager, and Frank Moores, the future premier of Newfoundland who was running a fish plant in the community at the time. From that meeting, it was decided that George would start a senior hockey team that would play out of the new arena.

The Conception Bay CeeBees were born.

That fall, Alex, who had been employed as a lineman with Newfoundland Light and Power, moved to Harbour Grace to work

Alex as an original member of the Conception Bay CeeBees in 1958. Pictured left to right are George Faulkner, Jimmy Kennedy and Alex. Kennedy was also from Bishop's Falls.

at Moores' fish plant and join the new team, which featured George as its playing coach.

A big difference for Alex and the rest of the CeeBee players was the amount of time they were able to spend on the ice in Harbour Grace. They would play shinny (pick-up hockey open to anyone) in the morning, and then George would put them through an hour-and-a-half practice every night. Up until then, Alex had only been practising a couple of times a week and playing just thirty games a year.

The extra ice time paid off for the CeeBees, who reached the finals in their first year and won the Herder in the second, 1959-60.

It also benefited Alex in a big way. Already dominant, he got better.

That fall, King Clancy was in the province visiting Howie Meeker, the former Toronto Maple Leafs player and coach who had moved to St. John's to run the United Church's hockey program at the newly-built Prince of Wales Arena in the centre of the city. During Clancy's visit, the CeeBees were in Town (as St. John's is called by folks outside it) playing a pre-season exhibition game against the Guards, a team Meeker was coaching. Alex and George had outstanding performances and caught Clancy's eye. A few days after the match, the brothers Faulkner got a call from Toronto.

After playing on the river all day, on Saturday nights, the Faulkner five would gather around the radio and faithfully listen to Toronto play. They would collect 8x10 pictures of Maple Leafs players by sending away the top of a cereal box and twenty-five cents. Alex could name almost every player who skated with the team during the 1940s and '50s.

The Maple Leafs wanted them to try out.

Still the property of the Canadiens, that wasn't an option for George, unless Montreal made a deal with Toronto for his rights. With that not going to happen, the older Faulkner instead focused his efforts on convincing Alex to take advantage of a once-in-a-lifetime opportunity. If nothing comes of it, the big brother would say, Alex could come back home after getting the opportunity to practice with the Leafs and meet the players.

The Leafs, after all, were the focus of the Faulkners' adoration when they were boys. After playing on the river all day, on Saturday nights, the Faulkner five would gather around the radio and faithfully listen to Toronto play. They would collect 8x10 pictures of Maple Leafs players by sending away the top of a cereal box and twenty-five cents. Alex could name almost every player who skated with the team during the 1940s and '50s.

After days of coaxing, Alex decided to go for it.

Once on the ice practising with the Leafs, Red Kelly approached him. After going from being one of the league's top defencemen with Detroit in the 1950s to a playmaking centre with Toronto, Kelly obviously knew what it took to get to the NHL and stay there. He offered Faulkner sage advice: Don't let any player think they're better than you, because they're not. The veteran also advised him to play with all the confidence he could muster. Faulkner was encouraged, and over-the-moon thrilled that a player of Kelly's stature would take the time to give such advice.

The practices George had been putting the CeeBees through in Harbour Grace helped Alex as he trained with Toronto that morning. From his experience in the Quebec league, George had adopted the drills being used in practice by the Montreal Canadiens.

So Faulkner was able to adapt to the Leafs' workout quite easily. His efforts during the practice impressed Imlach.

The general manager told Faulkner that he could likely play in the NHL if he spent a year-and-a-half honing his skills in the American Hockey League. It was the first time anyone had actually told Faulkner that he had a chance at making it to hockey's greatest stage.

Imlach's words were mind-boggling and surreal, but Faulkner was quite willing and determined to become a National Hockey League player, something no one from Newfoundland had accomplished since the league had started in 1917. Alex was offered a five-game tryout with Toronto's AHL team in Rochester, New York. The Leafs would put him up in a hotel and pay $200 a week, plus expenses. Imlach also told Faulkner that he could take as much time as he needed to play those five games, that he could practise until he felt comfortable and ready to see game action. And if Faulkner felt he needed more time after his first game, the Leafs' general manager told him to tell Rochester playing coach Steve Kraftcheck and then practise until he was ready for another game.

That was in early November.

Heeding Imlach's advice, Faulkner didn't play for the Americans for five or six weeks. As he practised with the pros, it was soon obvious to him that he needed to work on his conditioning. He was as fast as his well-conditioned teammates, but never had the legs or lungs to stay with them for a prolonged period.

He wasn't accustomed to lagging behind at any point of a game or practice.

In Newfoundland, he never had to catch anybody. Everybody had chased him. But if he was going to play professional hockey, he would have to get in good enough shape to stay at the front of the pack.

Drive and determination overtook Faulkner.

A non-drinker, he resisted getting involved in the party lifestyle some players enjoyed away from the rink. There were no distractions for him. He was in Rochester for one reason and one reason only – to get to the National Hockey League. He would work so hard during practice that his heart would be pounding and his head would be spinning when he stepped off the ice. There'd be no energy left to do anything else. He put himself through such punishment two hours a day, every day.

Besides his intense effort to become as well-conditioned as the other players, life in Rochester wasn't an easy transition for Faulkner. Unlike home, where everyone seemed to know everyone, he didn't know a soul in Rochester. He would walk the streets past hundreds of people without recognizing a face. And hearing a familiar voice wasn't much of an option. He had very little contact with home. Phone calls were rare at the time because of the cost. He only spoke with his parents a handful of times that winter. But he was too determined to play in the NHL to get homesick.

Being away from Newfoundland was just another hurdle he had to overcome for a shot at playing in the big league.

It would have been easier for him to pack it in, go home and say he had no intention of working that hard.

Minor pro hockey didn't fatten players' wallets in those days. Faulkner could make just as much, or more, working in Moores' fish plant as he did playing hockey. Plus, if he returned home, he could play in the senior league with the CeeBees and enjoy being a standout on the contending team.

But he wouldn't even consider those options.

Faulkner didn't want the question of, "What if I had stayed?" hanging over his head for the rest of his life. He could live with a coach or manager telling him he should go home because he wasn't going to make it. But he couldn't handle quitting and returning home to Newfoundland on his accord.

The weeks of hard work paid off once he felt ready to play. His first game action for the Americans came on December 25, 1960, against the Springfield Indians in Springfield.

On his first Christmas Day away from Bishop's Falls, Faulkner received a wonderful gift – the reassurance that he could play at the American Hockey League level. He came oh-so-close to scoring too, missing a goal by inches.

His next action came a few days later against the Quebec Aces.

Rochester played them twice in the old Quebec Colisee. Faulkner didn't miss the net in those games. He scored in both match-ups, with each of his first two professional goals coming against Gerry McNeil, a former NHL all-star who had led Montreal to two Stanley Cups in the previous decade.

With two goals in three games, Rochester didn't wait for Faulkner to complete his five-game tryout. The team offered him a professional contract and he quickly signed it. Faulkner would always view signing that first deal as the most important day of his professional career. He was excited and eager for the opportunity to challenge himself and find out if he was good enough for the National Hockey League.

This was a new dream. Faulkner had never made playing in the NHL a career goal. In fact, the high school drop-out had never really made any great plans.

He ended up playing forty-one games with Rochester in the 1960-61 season, receiving little ice time as the team's lines had already been set when he joined the team.

Despite his lack of playing time, he scored five goals and assisted on thirteen others for eighteen points. It wasn't a spectacular year offensively – especially considering the numbers he had been putting up back home in Newfoundland – but that rookie campaign laid the groundwork for much bigger things to come.

After staying in shape by playing soccer in St. John's with a team called the Fieldians all summer, Faulkner arrived at Toronto's training camp that September ready and raring to go. Although he didn't make the Leafs and was returned to Rochester, Imlach must have sensed Faulkner's hunger and felt that he had progressed a lot since that first practice with Toronto that previous November.

> He might have played a nondescript game, but it was history in the making. Wearing number eight, Faulkner was officially the first Newfoundlander to play in the National Hockey League.

On December 7, 1961, when Dave Keon, an all-star centre, was injured, Toronto called Faulkner up from their farm team for a game against the Canadiens, the Leafs' arch-rival. Alex was pleased, but not overly surprised because it was what he had been working towards. He knew, however, that he was only there in case someone got hurt, and he saw a few shifts in a 4-1 loss at the Montreal Forum.

He might have played a nondescript game, but it was history in the making. Wearing number eight, Faulkner was officially the first Newfoundlander to play in the National Hockey League.

And another Newfoundlander who would become synonymous with the league was there to witness it. Bob Cole, a broadcaster for VOCM at the time and the future play-by-play man with *Hockey Night in Canada*, had flown up from St. John's for the game.

Faulkner had been keeping him posted on every development in his hockey career, and this was the biggest of them all.

The achievement captured the imagination of Canada's youngest province, making headlines and many new fans.

It further fueled the determination of Faulkner. Although he had accomplished his goal and played in the NHL, it was only for a cup of coffee – as sportswriters call short stints in the big leagues.

Faulkner wanted to be a regular at the buffet.

He returned to Rochester with a new confidence. The guy, who not too long before had felt he lagged behind his American Hockey League teammates, was now staying at the front of the pack and becoming an offensive force. During his second season in Rochester, he led the Amerks in scoring, averaging more than a point per game on seventy-three points in sixty-five matches. He missed being one of the league's top ten scorers by just six points. (He likely would have been in the top ten if he hadn't missed six games because of a punch in the face from future NHL tough guy John Ferguson, then of the Cleveland Barons.)

Alex had reason to smile when this picture was taken after a game in the Stanley Cup finals. He had two goals in a 3-2 Detroit win over Toronto. It was the Red Wings only victory in the series. He was first star of the game on *Hockey Night in Canada.*

Faulkner's success that season was a reassurance that he could take his game to the next level. But it wouldn't be with Toronto.

Despite his offensive outburst in Rochester, the Leafs were deep with talent at the centre position and they left Faulkner off their protected list.

The Detroit Red Wings, however, scooped him up in the intraleague draft on June 4, 1962. He considered it a positive

While with Detroit, Alex (left) faced off against some of the greatest players in hockey history, including Bobby Hull.

development, accepting that it would have been next to impossible to crack the Leafs' roster.

He stayed fit by playing soccer over the summer and arrived at training camp in shape and ready to be a Red Wing. And become one he did, hustling his way onto a roster that featured legends like Gordie Howe, Alex Delvecchio and Terry Sawchuck.

Wearing number twelve – the number he wore back home playing for the CeeBees – he would centre Detroit's third line, with Bruce McGregor and Larry Jeffery on his wings.

Faulkner was finally a full-time National Hockey League player – much to his own delight and the joy of people back in Newfoundland where by now he had become a superhero.

Going from the American League to the NHL wasn't as big a jump as it was going from Harbour Grace to Rochester, but on more than one occasion, he would look at his teammates or opponents and be in awe of where he was. At times, he would even take a shift alongside Howe, the man widely considered the best hockey player in the world at the time.

It was all quite a thrill, but Faulkner's awe ended once the puck was dropped. When the game started, a player was just another player and a sheet of ice was a sheet of ice.

Faulkner played seventy games with Detroit in his rookie season, scoring ten goals and adding an equal number of assists.

His first goal came against Montreal and was something of a fluke. He had the puck behind the net and attempted to feed it out front to McGregor, but the pass went off Canadiens' back-up goaltender Cesare Maniago and into the net.

While that was a solid season for a rookie, Faulkner enjoyed greater success during the Wings' Stanley Cup playoff run. With Jefferey injured, coach Sid Abel put Andre Pronovost, a veteran forward who had won three Cups with Montreal, on the third line with Faulkner and McGregor. And in eight playoff games as part of that trio, Faulkner scored five goals, most on the team next to Howe, who had seven. Two of his markers were game-winners in the semi-finals against the Chicago Blackhawks and the legendary goaltender Glenn Hall. Two others, including another game-winner,

Alex (number twelve) fires during the 1963 Stanley Cup playoffs against the Toronto Maple Leafs. Also in the photo are future hockey hall of famers Johnny Bower (in goal), Tim Horton (in front of Faulkner) and Carl Brewer (top right corner).

came in one game, a 3-2 victory during the Stanley Cup finals against the Toronto Maple Leafs.

His performance in the only game Detroit would win in that series earned him the honour as the game's first star, and an interview on *Hockey Night in Canada* with Bobby Hull and Pierre Pilotte. It also created a frenzy in Newfoundland, where a wave of pride crashed against the shore and seemed to douse every man, woman and child.

He and Doris Reid, a woman from Botwood he had met, got married in Toronto immediately after the season ended and honeymooned in Florida. They actually couldn't afford to go home to Newfoundland, get hitched and then go to the Sunshine State – something else that is hard to fathom considering the salaries of today's players.

When he returned home, Faulkner was given a welcome reserved for royalty. There were not one or two, but three parades. The routes: Grand Falls to Botwood, Brigus to Harbour Grace, and on Water Street in St. John's, where there was a ticker tape procession and schools were closed due to Alex Faulkner Day. In Botwood, the crowd was so thick he wasn't able to drive away in a fire truck. It frightened Faulkner that he had to speak in front of so many people. And after the parade in St. John's, a reception was held and Premier Joey Smallwood presented Alex with gold cufflinks.

It was a welcome fit for a hockey hero.

Buoyed by his playoff performance, Faulkner was pumped when the next season started that fall. So were his many fans back in Newfoundland. Before his first game, he was presented with a good-luck telegram, containing thousands of signatures that would stretch from the blue line to the net four times.

Alex started the season on a torrid scoring streak, accumulating nine points in his first nine games. After one practice early that season, he came home and told his wife that he was finally feeling like he belonged, that he could play at the NHL level.

During a game not long after that, as he shot the puck into the opposing team's corner in a game against Toronto, Faulkner was bumped by Leafs defenceman Bobby Baun. The hit wasn't hard, just awkward. Faulkner's left hand nipped between Baun's body and his own leg, breaking the main bone in his third finger.

Six or so weeks on the disabled list didn't slow Faulkner's pace though. Upon returning, he had three points in three games, but then tore the ligaments from ankle to knee in a practice.

The second injury would be the lowest point in his hockey career. He would see action in eighteen more regular season games that year, but he failed to register a point in either of them.

And there was no encore of his playoff performance a year earlier. Faulkner suited up for four post-season games, but failed to register a point as the Wings came within a feather of winning the Stanley Cup.

Up three games to two, Detroit was ahead in game six with ten minutes to go, but Toronto tied it and went on to win in overtime on a goal by Baun. The Leafs then went on to capture the cup with a game seven victory.

The following season, the Red Wings asked Faulkner to begin the year in the minors. He opted to return to Newfoundland and play in Harbour Grace, where he would make more money than in

After his playoff performance in 1963, Faulkner received a telegram from Newfoundland at the start of the next season. It contained thousands of signatures.

the minor leagues. He won the scoring title that first season and the CeeBees remained a force in provincial senior hockey.

With NHL expansion on the horizon in 1967, Faulkner took another crack at pro hockey in the 1966-67 season. Six new teams were being added the following year – including Los Angeles,

Pittsburgh, Philadelphia, and St. Louis – and Faulkner figured the odds were good that he might get picked up.

Still the property of Detroit, he went back to the Red Wings' training camp that fall, with the hopes of having a good year in the minors and getting claimed in the expansion draft.

He spent the year with the Wings' farm team in Memphis and put up some impressive numbers. He had eighty-eight points in seventy games, leading his team in scoring and missing the Central Professional Hockey League's scoring title by just two points. He also had seven points in as many playoff games.

Still, despite such an offensive season, he didn't hear his name called in the expansion draft. The new teams selected lower-scoring teammates and players from other teams who hadn't put up the same kind of numbers Faulkner did. The likely reason why – because he had returned to Newfoundland for those two seasons instead of reporting to the minors as asked.

Not being picked up was disheartening, but he decided to stick with it and see if he could work his way onto an NHL team. Faulkner played the next three seasons with the San Diego Gulls in the Western Hockey League. Playing in a line-up that also featured his younger brother Jack in that first year, he had the third-most points on the team. He then finished fourth in Gulls' scoring following two seasons. He started another season in San Diego, but opted to head back to Newfoundland, where he finished his competitive playing days with the St. John's Capitals.

Faulkner would forever regret coming home for those two years, but not in a major way.

He had lived a dream and accomplished something most Newfoundlanders never thought imaginable in the early 1960s – he had cracked an NHL line-up.

No other Newfoundlander would play in the original, six-team league.

It would be five seasons after NHL expansion, and eleven years after Faulkner's first game, before Corner Brook's Joe Lundrigan got his shot with the Toronto Maple Leafs in the 1972-73 season.

When Riverhead, Harbour Grace native Dan Cleary of the Detroit Red Wings won the Stanley Cup and brought it to Newfoundland in the summer of 2008, he included Faulkner (left) in the large festivities.

Faulkner's accomplishment has often been remembered and lauded over the years. In the summer of 2008, for example, the then seventy-two-year-old was front and centre in a large celebration held for Daniel Cleary, the first Newfoundlander to win the Stanley Cup. (Fittingly, Cleary won the prize with the Detroit Red Wings.) A few weeks later, Alex was named third on the list of Newfoundland and Labrador's Ten Best Athletes, which was chosen by a sports panel and initiated by *The Telegram* in St. John's. (His brother George finished first, while Olympic medal-winning curler Brad Gushue was second.)

Fueled by a love of hockey, Faulkner reached the NHL through hard work, desire, determination and the ability to face fears. If he had let anxiety get the better of him as he walked to Maple Leaf Gardens for the first time, what some consider the biggest accomplishment in Newfoundland and Labrador sports history might never have happened.

CRAIG DOBBIN

ABOVE ITS SURFACE, especially when the sun is at a certain point and casting a golden light across the landscape, St. John's Harbour is stunningly picturesque. The vista includes historic Signal Hill, a slim gateway to the Atlantic aptly named The Narrows, and a jellybean-like collection of clapboard homes built on a craggy shore known as The Battery. But it's a different story beneath the hazel-tinted waters of a port that's been a hub of commerce since the 1500s. For more than a century, much to the ire of many, the harbour has been a place to flush human waste. Its waters look, and quite often smell, revolting.

Even though some of North America's earliest business transactions took place there 500 years ago, as the English, French, Portuguese and Spanish bartered codfish, because of today's pollution, it's now hardly a place that fills the eye with dollar signs. When the wind is a certain way, people are too busy plugging their noses to sense opportunity. But forty or so years ago, a near miss on the bottom of murky St. John's Harbour spurred an entrepreneurial awakening like few Canada has ever seen.

While running an underwater salvage business, a commercial diver named Craig Dobbin found himself in trouble on the harbour floor. Something had gone seriously wrong with his scuba gear. "I was out of air, had lead boots and no lifeline," he later recalled. Dobbin promised to find a better way to make a living – if he survived. But not only did he rise from the depths and live a better life, he soared, quite literally, from the disgusting depths of St. John's Harbour to the top of the business world.

Dobbin built CHC Helicopters, the world's largest helicopter service, over an almost thirty-year period and earned a reputation as one of the greatest risk takers the Canadian business world has ever seen. He regularly took gambles – some that paid off and others that didn't. He befriended powerful and influential men. And he became a philanthropist, giving to organizations publicly, and to needy individuals privately. While doing all this, he overcame adversities as daunting as his underwater ordeal, surviving a helicopter crash and a lung transplant. It's fitting that one of his favourite sayings over the years became, "Turn adversity into opportunity."

Craig Laurence Dobbin was born on Friday the 13th in September 1935. It's not a lucky date for the superstitious, and it wasn't the most fortunate era to be born in Newfoundland. St. John's and the rest of Newfoundland faced severe poverty and political uncertainty. The Great Depression of the 1930s was ravaging the fishing, forestry and mining industries. Many of the unemployed found themselves on what was known as the dole, meagre government food allotments that only provided a portion of a person's nutritional requirements. As well, two years prior to Dobbin's birth, the Dominion of Newfoundland had succumbed to the weight of not being able to pay off a debt that had grown dramatically because of the First World War. Newfoundland, the country, handed over rule to what was called the Commission of Government, which took office in early 1934.

Dobbin was the third of Rita (Power) and Patrick Dobbin's eleven children. He attended Catholic schools in St. John's, getting his early education at St. Pat's and graduating from St. Bonaventure's College, or St. Bon's as it is still known. There were two Paddy Dobbins in St. John's at the time, Black Paddy and Red Paddy. Craig's father was Red Paddy because of his red hair and beard. For years, Red Paddy ran a lumberyard for Harvey and Company, but he later branched out on his own, opening PJ Dobbin Lumber and Building Supplies.

It was while helping his father in the small lumberyard, which was located on Torbay Road, when Craig learned some valuable, rough-and-tumble business lessons. The labour was hard. He would load lumber and take it to clients in places like St. Mary's, about an hour from St. John's. After he'd unload it, he'd rush back to town to put the money in the bank to help the company make payroll. The job taught him a lot about the importance of cash flow, margins and customer service.

> Dobbin built CHC Helicopters, the world's largest helicopter service, over an almost thirty-year period and earned a reputation as one of the greatest risk takers the Canadian business world has ever seen.
>
>

Dobbin's first salaried job was as a clerk with the U.S. army base at Fort Pepperrell in St. John's. He also got into commercial diving, doing things like underwater demolition, salvage and recovery. The latter included recovering bodies. Down the road, he would joke that he couldn't eat lobster because he had pulled so many bodies out of the ocean with the crustaceans eating them.

Obviously, diving wasn't what he wanted to do. His epiphany at the bottom of St. John's Harbour, combined with the fact he and his wife had had five kids in six years and for the first couple did not have a washing machine or refrigerator, made him want a way out. He started building houses and, in the early days before he could afford a pickup, is said to have driven around in an old car with no windshields. He would carry materials in it, with lumber sticking out of the front and rear.

The Dobbins moved a lot. Once Craig started a dwelling, he'd move his family in as soon as it was livable. They would stay there until another was habitable. The word "habitable" is used loosely here. In more than one house, the Dobbin kids would reach their bedrooms by climbing a ladder because stairs were not installed. Mark Dobbin, Craig's oldest son, remembers trying to get some sleep during the summer months only to be awoken by the sounds of a carpenter's hammer hitting the wall of the next room. "Mom said she got to the point where she was afraid to take me down to the Janeway (children's hospital)," he laughs. "I had a couple of bad falls as a kid opening the basement stairs and falling down to the freshly installed slab because there was no stairs installed yet."

But those unfinished stairs were the first steps in the creation of a significant and successful real estate company. Dobbin formed Craig Dobbin Limited in 1963 and Omega Investments Limited in 1966. He expanded into subdivisions and apartment units, including Hillview Terrace, an East End St. John's complex located off Torbay Road on land city hall had once expropriated from his father. It apparently always stuck in Dobbin's throat that the city had taken the land for development, but sat on it for years before selling it to him for profit. He wasn't bitter about a lot of things, but the injustice of the expropriation is said to have always rankled him.

Dobbin landed deals to build the Kmart stores in St. John's. Omega built the super department stores on Topsail and Torbay Roads, and obviously pleased with Dobbin, the owners of the growing chain, the Kresge Corporation, recruited him to build stores in Montreal, Ottawa and other places. It appears he got Kmart construction down to a science and was putting them up in thirty-eight or forty days.

Not one to ignore opportunity, Craig also started building apartment complexes and taking on other projects while working in Montreal and Ottawa. It got to the point where most of his business was there and, in 1968, he moved to Ottawa. The family would spend three years in the city and, not surprisingly, lived in a couple of houses. The Dobbins then moved to Montreal where they spent a few years before returning to St. John's in 1974.

Some time in the early 1970s, Dobbin befriended Frank Duff Moores, the man who had knocked Joey Smallwood out of the Newfoundland premier's chair in 1971. They shared interests and spent a lot of time socializing and playing cards. Moores also introduced Dobbin to salmon fishing, and that led the businessman to a new passion and industry. As premier, Moores had access to a government helicopter and would use it on occasion to reach some of the province's more isolated and fish-filled pools. Hooked on the sport, and more than happy to spend ten or twelve hours at a time on a river, Dobbin wanted his own helicopter so he could cast a fly where and when he wanted. In 1976, he bought a Hughes 500D, a light utility helicopter originally built because the US army wanted a craft for light observation. The bird cost Dobbin in the vicinity of $100,000, and although it got him to prime salmon locations, he was soon reminded the fishing season wasn't that long and maintaining a helicopter wasn't cheap. In fact, it was costing him almost as much to operate it as it did to buy it. The numerous costs included renting a hangar, paying pilots, maintenance and insurance.

Dobbin approached Universal Helicopters, which was then owned by Okanagan Helicopters. He tried to strike a deal, offering them the opportunity to maintain, staff and make profit from it throughout the year. He just wanted to use it during the five or six weeks of the fishing season. It seemed like a decent deal to Dobbin, but the company rejected it, apparently in an arrogant and high-handed fashion. Dobbin looked elsewhere and discovered that there were no other commercial helicopter companies flying in the province. Viewing any company that was arrogant and had a monopoly as a business opportunity, he decided to enter the helicopter business. Licenses were not being given to new operators at the time, so he started searching for an existing one. He found Gem Air, a small, Winnipeg-based helicopter company that he ended up buying. Dobbin had no idea at the time, but Gem Air would be the first of many helicopter companies he would purchase.

Dobbin moved the operating license back to Newfoundland. He hired management and re-christened the company Sealand Helicopters. The firm started seeking work and soon won a five-year contract for Newfoundland's air ambulance services. The company also found itself doing a lot of work for Mobil Oil Canada, which was exploring a burgeoning oilfield named Hibernia.

If getting into the helicopter business was a risk for Dobbin, in August 1979, he gained first-hand insight into exactly how hazardous it could be. While flying a few hundred kilometres from St. John's, and with a couple of bankers and the president of Memorial University on board, the helicopter's engine died and the emergency auto-rotation cut in. The machine approached power lines, the pilot aborted the flight, and they crashed in a wooded area. The pilot and one of the bankers were killed. Everyone else on board was injured, including Dobbin who, despite broken bones, managed to find the nearby railbed and walked until he found help.

Instead of being turned off from helicopters because of the tragedy, Dobbin pressed on with a greater appreciation and commitment to safety. He took a flight within a week of being let out of hospital, and even had the pilot perform stunts to get him back in the game. Incidentally, Dobbin never learned to operate a helicopter himself. He maintained it would be too hard to do that and entertain at the same time. He loved helicopters, not the technology, but the opportunities they could open up.

Sealand was hired to provide helicopter services to companies exploring for oil off the coast of Newfoundland. Even though he was struggling to meet its payroll at the time, Dobbin sensed greater opportunity in the offshore and purchased a fleet of Super Puma helicopters. Sealand was the first company on the continent to have the machines and the purchase made it a player.

Photos courtesy of The Telegram

Dobbin loved helicopters and the opportunity they represented. He felt they could open up the world.

With oil exploration work off Newfoundland slowing down in the 1980s, Dobbin realized his home province had a limited market for helicopter work. In 1987, he began assembling a company which became CHC Helicopter Corporation and would be known simply as "CHC" or "Canadian Helicopters." He created it by combining Sealand with four other companies — Toronto, Viking, Ranger, and Okanagan, the company that had launched him into the industry by shunning his offer to use and maintain his fishing toy ten years earlier. CHC became publicly traded on the Toronto Stock Exchange in 1987. It wasn't the greatest time to go public. On October 19, known as Black Monday, panic ripped through the world's financial industry as the stock markets experienced their largest percentage decline in history. The Toronto exchange saw a 22.5 per cent drop that day. CHC, which had raised $44 million in its initial public offering just before the crash, persevered. The turbulence didn't stop it from taking off.

Dobbin started looking at global business opportunities. He also continued buying smaller helicopter companies, including Ranger Helicopters Canada and Maple Leaf. By 1990, CHC's fleet had grown to 256 helicopters, and the company was operating in more than a dozen countries.

In the early nineties, the company branched out into different areas, such as providing United Nations peacekeeping flights throughout Kuwait, Cambodia and Thailand and getting into the helicopter repair business through the purchase of existing companies in other countries.

In 1993, Dobbin struck a deal that would pay huge dividends to the company and his family. To operate in Europe he needed European citizenship. Boasting his Irish heritage and using his considerable negotiating skills, he managed to reach what he considered one of his best deals yet. In return for funding a chair in Canadian studies at the University of Ireland, he got dual Irish/Canadian passports for himself, and then in 2001 for his five children, as well as an honourary degree. The status secured the company's growth in Europe and boosted its succession plan.

Dobbin considered the investment in the Irish university some of the best money he had ever spent.

The beginning of the nineties also saw Dobbin enter another aviation industry. He founded Air Atlantic, a regional commercial airline in Atlantic Canada. This risk didn't pay off like the helicopter business. Air Atlantic accumulated a lot of debt, and Dobbin sold it to the Halifax-based IMP Group in the fall of 1995. The bumps felt by the burgeoning airline, however, didn't make Dobbin fly any lower. In 1994, he negotiated another major acquisition for CHC, buying British International Helicopters.

A lung transplant and number of near-misses didn't stop Dobbin's ascent in the business world.

At the same time all this was happening in the early 1990s, Dobbin was diagnosed with idiopathic pulmonary fibrosis. It's a rare disease that causes lung tissue to scar, taking away the ability of that tissue to transfer oxygen to the bloodstream. Coincidentally, the condition also ran in his second wife Elaine's family. Dobbin was slowly losing his capacity to breathe. "The doctors said I had four months to live unless I got myself a new lung," he said. "That's when I decided death was not an option."

Dobbin sized up the location of North American hospitals and placed himself smack in the middle of the US at Birmingham, Alabama. It was the city with the highest concentration of hospitals two hours away by jet. Because of that, he was able to get himself listed as a local resident at ten of those hospitals. Due to Dobbin's 6'3" height, it was difficult to find donors with matching lungs. His condition grew worse and he reached the point where he couldn't breathe without a face mask.

Eventually, in 1997, he got his new lungs in Philadelphia at the University of Pennsylvania Hospital – the oldest medical school in the United States. He arrived at the Philadelphia operating room two hours and ten minutes after he got the call. "It was a very hard chore," he said of the operation, "but the thought never ever entered my mind that I wouldn't be able to repair the inconvenience that was prohibiting me from having a full life."

And have a full life Dobbin did. Instead of taking his foot off the gas and slowing his pace a little, he went full throttle. In 1998, he spun off a helicopter maintenance and repair company called Vector Aerospace through a public offering, and then pushed CHC to even greater heights. "I've come to grips with the finality of life," he said in a 1999 interview. "I'm sixty-four and I feel nineteen. I'm very grateful for every day I have...If I felt any better, you'd have to tie me down." Dobbin didn't just survive a lung transplant, his friend Leo Barry would say years later, "He prospered."

In June 1999, Dobbin bought up yet another competitor. This time it was Helicopter Services Group of Norway, for which he paid $207 million. The purchase was scrutinized by regulators who feared that CHC would have too much control in the industry. But the deal passed, making CHC the largest helicopter operating firm on the planet. "I should tell you we made a hell of buy, we got it at a good price and we got a good company," Dobbin said.

The purchase of Helicopter Services Group paid immediate dividends for CHC. Earnings in the quarter following the deal quadrupled over the same three-month period a year earlier. Around the same time, the company expanded other areas of its operation, such as opening CHC Composites in Gander. That subsidiary made parts for the Cormorant helicopter.

Dobbin had long been grooming his kids for a life in business. He would never sit down and lecture them. But he would let them sit in on the business meetings he often held at home with prospective partners, clients or bankers. His children would sit quietly and listen. If they opened their mouth uninvited, they were asked to leave. It provided them with a great education in commerce at an early age.

A risky business practice Dobbin appeared to have taught himself, and mastered by the time CHC bought Helicopter Services Group, was the art of leveraging, or borrowing money to invest. He would borrow to continue the company's growth, much to the amazement of his less risk-inclined friends and foes. For one deal, Dobbin was able to convince the CEO of the Bank of Nova Scotia, Peter Godsoe, to loan him a whopping $750 million. Dobbin once told a CBC reporter that if they compared bank accounts, the journalist would have more. "What I do with my money, I use it to lever up to a bigger pie," he said. "I take all my money and lever it up. I've been doing that since high school."

In his business dealings, Dobbin didn't just use his tolerance for risk; he also relied on his engaging personality. The phrase "larger than life" has been used to describe him by countless people. Once while in Norway, for instance, Dobbin was asked to attend a swanky function in honour of an offshore company's tenth anniversary. He was asked to speak and bring greetings from Newfoundland. Cleverly, that afternoon he asked a sauna attendant to write a speech in Norwegian. They worked through it and Dobbin later toasted the company and the youth of Norway and Newfoundland to great applause. "It was not simply an act of politeness," friend and sometimes business partner Cabot Martin wrote in an article for *The Independent*, "he galvanized the room."

With such wit and charm, it's no surprise that people liked being around Dobbin, and he had an ability to form friendships that lasted a lifetime. His friends came from all walks of life, from the rich and powerful to the poor and troubled. His long-time friends included Moores, former Prime Minister Brian Mulroney and Harry Steele, another legendary Newfoundland businessman. Late in life, he befriended former US president George H.W. Bush. They only saw each other two or three times a year, but corresponded regularly. Bush actually made international headlines when he fell in a bog during a visit to a Dobbin fishing lodge in Labrador in the early nineties.

One telling story of Dobbin's ability to make friends involved Canadian hair and beauty product magnate Steve Hudson. When Hudson worked for Newcourt Credit Group in the 1990s, Dobbin had defaulted on some of the payments for the Dash 8s he had leased for Air Atlantic through the financing company. Hudson came to the airport in St. John's to seize the planes, but was unable to find them, as Dobbin moved them from hangar to hangar. Dobbin contacted Hudson after a couple of days and suggested that they settle the dispute over an Irish whiskey. They became fast friends.

Still, even though he was a fun and lovable guy, Dobbin was far from being a soft touch when it came to running CHC or striking business deals. He considered himself a casting director rather than a business master. While he tried to make the people he cast feel like family, he also had expectations of them. His grasp of deadlines and responsibilities often made him a difficult taskmaster. Dobbin is said to have had a number of different techniques he used with his employees and the people who did business with him. If he had a problem and wanted to solve it, he'd make it their problem. As someone who regularly bought up the competition, took risks and dealt his way to the top, Dobbin definitely stepped on some toes and made some enemies. Despite that, he didn't appreciate it when people would lump him in with greedy business people. "I don't like the term shark, because it's kind of demeaning," he once said. "I consider myself an entrepreneur, and I'm a credible, honest entrepreneur."

While he enjoyed clout in business, Dobbin also wielded a lot of power politically, particularly at home in Newfoundland. When he spoke, people and politicians listened.

With the company flying high, in 2002 Dobbin and CHC reached another milestone, becoming the first company based in Atlantic Canada to list on the New York Stock Exchange. On

October 12, with a red and blue CHC helicopter parked outside the stock exchange's building and a large contingent of colleagues and family watching, Dobbin rang the bell to open that day's trading. "It's a great day for all of us," he said. "It's the combination of twenty-five years of hard work." His only complaint, according to an interview in *The Telegram*, was the tea. "They can't make tea in New York."

Canadian Helicopters kept on climbing. In December 2003, months after the company restructured its board to meet new corporate governance regulations, CHC announced it had bought yet another competitor, Schreiner Aviation of the Netherlands. It was the leading offshore helicopter service company in the Dutch part of the North Sea, as well as a key player in the Nigerian offshore industry. The deal, Dobbin explained in an interview with the CBC, gave the company a presence in countries where it currently wasn't operating. "This is a perfect fit for CHC," Dobbin said. "The acquisition will significantly increase the international diversity of our operations."

While he enjoyed clout in business, Dobbin also wielded a lot of power politically, particularly at home in Newfoundland. When he spoke, people and politicians listened. He was heard often throughout his career, and at no time did his words resonate more than in February 2003. While addressing an oil and gas conference in St. John's, he offered his opinion on a host of issues affecting his homeland. He ranged from the province's image in the rest of Canada to the royalties it gets from its offshore oil. With two provincial cabinet ministers sitting at the same head table, he said the province's politicians were mediocre and criticized them for creating short-term jobs in an effort to get re-elected. Dobbin called for a revision of Newfoundland and Labrador's terms of union with Canada. People in the province need to take a look at the way their government is organized, he suggested. And he noted that the province made more money from licensing cars than from its offshore oil that year. "Unless Canada has some inherent need for a poor cousin, there's no need to refuse our request," he said. "We want the tools to become

Dobbin admitted he was trying to shock people in a 2003 speech that was highly critical of Newfoundland and Labrador's politicians.

equal, paying partners – nothing more." Dobbin also suggested the people of the province need to become masters of their own destiny. (This was a theme that appears to have been adopted by future premier Danny Williams's government some years later.)

After the explosive speech, which received a standing ovation, Dobbin admitted he was trying to push people's buttons. "I want to shock the existing politicians and people who want to come into politics," he said. "I want to shock Newfoundlanders into realizing what's happening – that our youth are gone, our outport way of life is decimated." An editorial in *The Telegram* the Saturday after the Thursday speech noted Dobbin's continued penchant for politics. "Craig Dobbin has always had a nose for politics, a gentle feel for the political barometer in a very political province. In his business, it's been as much a survival tool as being able to stare down the banks or wrestle the nastiest of competitors into submission."

Dobbin may have been a shrewd businessman and not short of an opinion when it came to Newfoundland and her politics, but he also gave to countless causes – medical research, minor basketball teams, seniors homes – and almost everything in between. He was often honoured for his giving, and the Canadian Society of Fundraising Executives' outstanding individual philanthropist award was among the acknowledgments. His Beachy Cove home became the site of many fundraising dinners and events for charities and non-profit organizations, and he also helped an untold number of individuals in need. "Craig was a great philanthropist," friend and former Newfoundland premier Brian Tobin said after his passing. "He contributed to many high-profile, public causes, and at the same time quietly lent a helping hand to many whose [poor] health or financial situation became known to him."

Craig and Elaine were strong supporters of the Autism Society of Newfoundland and Labrador. In December 2005, he donated $500,000 for the construction of a provincial autism facility. It was a third of a $1.5 million capital campaign for the facility. Elaine chaired that drive and the centre was named after her in June 2006. "My little sweetheart, he's very generous, what can I say? You know, he's blown me away with this," she told *The Telegram* after the half-million dollar donation.

In 2004, Dobbin stepped aside and let his long-time right-hand man Sylvain Allard take over as chief executive officer of CHC, although he retained the title of executive chairman. The move, analysts said, was designed to loosen some of Dobbin's grip on the company. Two thousand and four was also the year when Dobbin moved CHC's head office from St. John's to Vancouver, something that raised some eyebrows given Dobbin's renowned love of Newfoundland. Dobbin would have preferred to build a bigger office in St. John's and move staff there, but the company's management decided that wasn't the wise choice, considering CHC's customers and employees were spread throughout the world. The move didn't hurt the company financially. Fueled by high oil prices, in October CHC's shares edged slightly past $50 on the Toronto Stock Exchange. The company soon boasted its best quarter since going public. Net earnings were at ninety-eight cents a share, up thirty-seven cents from the year before. Besides moving CHC headquarters to the other end of the country, Dobbin also sold his long-held rental properties in St. John's – the ones he held for decades under Omega Investments – to an Alberta company for a reported thirty-five million dollars.

By now, Dobbin's dealmaking ability had become the stuff of legends. While those skills were often applied in boardrooms, over a drink or on a salmon river, Dobbin showcased them for the people of his hometown in late 2004 after he and his brother Derm landed a Quebec Major Junior Hockey franchise for St. John's. Once the brothers got the team, which they called the St. John's Fog Devils, they had to negotiate an arena usage deal with St. John's Sports and Entertainment, the operators of Mile One Stadium. But that organization had also bid on a Quebec league franchise but lost to the Dobbins. Talks between the two didn't go well, with Derm even walking away at one point. That move resulted in league president Gilles Courteau suspending the Fog Devils operation for a year. But at the 11th hour, after Courteau told the Dobbins there was still a window of opportunity to pull something off, Craig stepped in and negotiated a deal in hours. "He's my partner," Derm told *The Telegram* after the fact, "and when you need a big hitter, your cleanup hitter, you put in the best. That's who came in and he did it." (As a postscript, the Fog Devils began playing in the 2005-06 season, but would be gone after the 2007-08 campaign. The Dobbins sold the team to a businessman in the Montreal area.)

But while it appeared to the business world that Dobbin was starting to step back, he showed shareholders and the public that he had no plans to retire or loosen his grasp on CHC. In the spring of 2006, Dobbin, already the controlling shareholder, showed an interest in buying the company outright. The negotiations between Dobbin and two equity firms failed and the deal wasn't completed.

Dobbin's health started declining in the months that followed. On September 27, he managed to make it to CHC's annual shareholder meeting, where Mark was elected deputy chairman.

Business commentators said it was a sign the family was still in control. Dobbin took a leave of absence a few days later on October 6 and passed away at his home in Beachy Cove the next day. He was seventy-one and, through risk-taking and deal-making, had built a global empire. At the time of his death, CHC's annual revenues surpassed the $1 billion mark. The company had 3,400 employees and was operating more than 250 helicopters in thirty-five countries.

The tributes were plentiful after his death. They came from his many long-time friends in St. John's as well as the powerful people he had befriended over his career. Dobbin was remembered for his love of life – and things like cards and fishing – as well as for his entrepreneurial spirit and constant drive to succeed. "His determination was his main characteristic," friend and former federal cabinet minister John Crosbie said. "He was always moving forward and pushing to go further and advance his business."

Dobbin's funeral on October 9, 2006, attracted more than 3,000 people from all walks of life. The service at the Basilica in St. John's was attended by family and friends, business people and politicians from Newfoundland and Labrador as well as other provinces, including Quebec premier Jean Charest. There were tributes from his grandchildren and friends. George Bush was among them. He was unable to attend but sent a message that was read during the ceremony. Friend Harry Steele delivered the eulogy. "Business was the field," Steele said. "He played for his oversized personality, and by the way, not everyone from Beachy Cove gets invited to ring the opening bell at the New York Stock Exchange. Time spent in his company went faster, the laughter was louder, and he had this great Newfoundland gift of taking on life as if it was made for him. I'm a happy and better person to have known Craig Dobbin."

Less than a month after his passing, St. John's city council named the street leading to the airport after the entrepreneur. Fittingly, it was christened "Craig Dobbin's Way." And early the next summer, Dobbin was inducted into the Canadian Aviation Hall of Fame posthumously. He joined World War I flying ace

Steve Bartlett photo

The road leading to the St. John's International Airport was named after Dobbin just weeks after he passed away. People who did business with the tough yet charming negotiator might think the street's name fitting.

Billy Bishop and Canadian astronaut Chris Hadfield in the shrine, which is based in Wetaskiwin, Alberta.

These honours added to the many Dobbin had amassed during his rise in the helicopter business. He was the recipient of honourary degrees from St. Mary's University, The University College Dublin and Memorial University of Newfoundland. He was awarded the Medaille de l'Aeronautique, an honour given by France to people who have distinguished themselves in the development of aviation. He served as Ireland's consul general in Newfoundland and Labrador and as chair of the Ireland-Canada University Foundation in Dublin. At the turn of the century, Dobbin was feted with the distinction as Newfoundland's Businessman of the Millennium and, to no surprise, was inducted to the province's business hall of fame. Of all the honours and accolades, the Order of Canada, which he received in 1992, was the acknowledgment he most treasured.

Mark was appointed chair of CHC after his father's passing. He told the Canadian Press that his dad may have driven the company's growth but he also worked towards the day when he wouldn't be around. "My father was the consummate entrepreneur and built the company essentially from scratch, whereas I'm coming in much more in a capacity of taking an existing company and hopefully continuing to grow it," Mark said. "It's a different time for the company right now and a different set of challenges and in many ways I've been preparing for this eventuality for a long period of time."

In February 2008, it was announced that First Reserve Corp, an American private equity firm, was buying CHC for $3.7 billion. Some might say it is fitting that a company built on mergers was itself being taken over. It's impossible to know what Dobbin would have thought of the deal, or if it would have happened at all if he were still alive. One thing is for sure: if he were around, Dobbin would have persevered with wit and determination, just as he had done on that dark day while sitting on the bottom of St. John's Harbour. "If you are an entrepreneur in the true sense of the word, you are not taking any risks. You are simply executing a plan of which you are positive of the results," he told graduating MUN students upon receiving his honourary degree. "Dare to dream. Turn adversity into opportunity. Don't forget your reality check...But most importantly, have fun in life – it's a quick trip."

Craig Dobbin is often remembered for his tolerance for risk, his determination, and his larger-than-life personality.

MYRA BENNETT

IT'S IMPOSSIBLE TO imagine Myra Grimsley's first thoughts when she landed at Daniel's Harbour in the spring of 1921. The community on Newfoundland's Northern Peninsula had about 200 residents, one business and no roads, just paths. It was a world away from the post-world war London the thirty-one-year-old had just left. That city and its outlying areas had a population of seven million-plus, along with modern factories and streets of all sizes, including new arterials.

Socially and economically, Daniel's Harbour and London couldn't have been farther apart.

There wasn't even a proper wharf at Daniel's Harbour where the ship carrying her, a small coastal steamer called the *S.S. Home*, could dock. It had to anchor about a mile offshore. To disembark, Myra had to climb down a ladder that dangled over the side of the vessel. When the ship rolled with a wave, the ladder rose and she jumped into a waiting dory.

And after she got to shore, according to her son Trevor, there's a good chance she had to weave her way around a beach lined with rotting seal carcasses. She had arrived on May 27, after all, which would be smack dab in the middle of the annual seal harvest.

Seals or no seals, the whole experience had to be startling for Myra. But there was no looking back. She had committed to spending two years in Daniel's Harbour as the nurse for a 200-mile region spanning from Sally's Cove in the south and ended at Eddie's Cove West to the north.

Photos courtesy of the Bennett family
Myra as a young nurse.

Even though she had arrived to provide much-needed and long overdue health services, the people of Daniel's Harbour paid little attention to her the day she landed. It had been a late spring and the *Home* – which ran from Humbermouth, now part of Corner Brook, to Battle Harbour, Labrador – was about three weeks late in making its first run of the year. Provisions were overdue. After enduring an extra-long winter and running their stores low, the people were more focused on food than on the arrival of a petite Englishwoman who would directly or indirectly touch all of their lives, often over and over again.

Born in London on April Fool's Day in 1890, Myra Maud Grimsley was the second child of Steve and Patty Ellen Grimsley (nee Crapper). The couple would have nine children, with one son and two daughters dying in childhood. Steve was an interior decorator. Patty Ellen was a housewife with a humanitarian heart.

Patty Ellen planted seeds of compassion in Myra and the rest of her children at an early age. A generous person who always put others before her own family, she would assist people who lived in the slums of London and often take in strangers who fell upon hard times. Even though the Grimsleys were far from wealthy, Patty Ellen would feed the less fortunate first and then get something for herself and her family afterwards.

(Interestingly, while Patty Grimsley gave comfort to some of London's poor, her brother, Thomas Crapper, provided a little luxury to most of the world. According to Trevor, he invented the flush toilet and had to change his name for obvious reasons.)

Young Myra breezed through school, with a lot of help and support from her dad, who would sit at the kitchen table and help with her lessons. At ten, she was awarded a medal by Queen Victoria for punctuality and attendance. By thirteen, she had completed the required grades. Because the compulsory school-leaving age was fourteen, she spent her final year assisting children who had trouble with their lessons.

> A generous person who always put others before her own family, she would assist people who lived in the slums of London and often take in strangers who fell upon hard times.

After wrapping up her studies, Myra went to work for a German Jewish tailor on Saville Row, the London street that has been famous for its garment makers since the 1730s. There she trained as a tailor and developed a sewing skill that would serve her, and many others, well in the future. Myra helped make clothing for many of England's finest, including members of the Royal Family. She also continued her mother's tradition of helping the less fortunate, making garments for poor people who had nothing on their backs.

Around the same time, she got involved with a mission where, among other things, she taught Bible studies and did some sewing. Through the mission, which also dealt with the sick, there arose the opportunity for Myra to help medically and become a nurse. She pursued the profession, and acquired nursing skills at a couple of hospitals, including one in North

London where she received maternity training. Relying on her sewing skills, she also made her first nurse's uniform.

In her early twenties, Myra became a district nurse in the town of Woking, which was over twenty miles west of central London. (If the name sounds familiar, Woking was the town where Martians landed in H. G. Wells' 1898 science fiction classic *The War of the Worlds*.) Nursing in the railway junction town involved making house calls by foot or by bike.

The challenge of Myra's work increased with the beginning of World War I, when Britain declared war on Germany on August 4, 1914. A lot of medical personnel, including most doctors, were recruited to go to the front – the site of battle – and provide support for the troops. That meant nurses like Myra had to pick up the slack and carry out a lot of the duties doctors normally did.

Adding to the pressure were the increasing numbers of refugees arriving in London and the shortage of food in the city. The latter is one of the few aspects of the war Myra would

Myra (on the right in the back row) with a group of fellow nurses.

talk about in the years that followed. She would occasionally recollect to family members about how hungry everyone was during the war and how they would have to stand in line for rations.

The wartime efforts of nurses like Myra were complicated by the threat of German air attacks. Cigar-shaped Zeppelins started bombing the coast of England in January 1915 and hit London for the first time that May. These air raids continued regularly after that. There were almost 160 attacks, killing over 500 people and causing millions of pounds in damage. Sirens would signal an attack, although Myra would always know when one was imminent because dogs would howl and bark beforehand.

Because of the war, and the threat of air raids, London was put under blackout, meaning no lights could be seen at night. The darkness made it more dangerous and difficult for Myra to get around. In fact, there was at least one occasion where she ignored the blackout and found herself staring at a soldier's bayonet. Some locals came to her rescue, telling the soldier, "That's our nurse!"

In 1915, Myra moved on from Woking and went to work as a case worker in a maternity hospital in North London where she earned a certificate in midwifery, a skill she also applied in London's slums. There, in addition to delivering babies, she treated injured soldiers when they came home from the front and cared for refugees. After three years as a case worker, the nurse applied her skills as nurse in a home for unwed mothers.

The war years also saw Myra come down with the Spanish flu. She became very ill and remained extremely weak for a long time. She couldn't even push her bike around to get from house to house. The disease took a lot out of her, but she eventually rebounded.

Although she didn't know it, sewing, doing the work of doctors, delivering babies, and experiencing hunger and sickness firsthand all helped prepare Myra for the life she would lead in remote Daniel's Harbour.

The war also took a personal toll, as four of Myra's brothers were involved in the Allied effort and one of them was killed at Gallipoli. She also lost a good friend to the battle. Some time after the war ended November 11, 1918, Myra read a story in *Nursing World*. It was about a man in Saskatchewan, Canada, who had left home to get help for his pregnant wife, but didn't return in time and found both her and child dead. As if she had heard the man grieving – and perhaps because of the toll World War I had taken on her – Myra's missionary spirit was awoken and she applied to serve with the Overseas Nursing Association. It was recruiting nurses to work throughout the British Empire and she asked to be sent to Saskatchewan. But the organization told her it would be some time before it could get her to Canada. Berths on ships between Canada and England were scarce after the war ended.

Myra (top left) en route from England with some of the other nurses recruited to serve in Newfoundland.

Myra used the interim to further her training. She did another course in midwifery and also one in anaesthesia. Lady Alice Grey, the widow of the late Canadian Governor General Earl Grey, found her application and approached her about working in Canada. But, again, she would have to wait. There was still no way to get her across the Atlantic Ocean.

Lady Grey introduced Myra to Lady Constance Harris. She was the wife of Sir Alexander Harris, then governor of Newfoundland, a British dominion that had long been a valuable colony because of its lucrative fishery. After seeing first-hand the serious need for health services in rural areas of the island, Lady Harris was spearheading a program called the Outport Nursing Scheme and had travelled to England to recruit nurses. She wanted Myra to be part of the initiative, which would lead to the Newfoundland Outport Nursing and Industrial Association. She explained to the nurse that there were no berths to Canada, but there were to Newfoundland. Myra, her missionary spirit still strong despite the two-year wait, said yes, as long as the need was there.

The pay was $1,000 a year.

On Friday, April 13, 1921, Myra boarded a ship and left London with three other Lady Harris had recruited to act as nurses and midwives in Newfoundland's outports. She was excited. They crossed the Atlantic and sailed into St. John's, the dominion's capital city, ten days later. The other nurses were dispatched to Burgeo on the southwest coast, Fogo Island just off the northeast coast, and Hant's Harbour on the Avalon Peninsula.

Myra, because of her vast experience, was assigned to the remotest region of the island, the Northern Peninsula. After a few weeks in St. John's and a stopover in Curling, Grimsley finally boarded the *S.S. Home* for Daniel's Harbour. Having heard that the nurse was on the passenger boat, people in Cow Head, a community 30 miles south of Daniel's Harbour, greeted the ship and asked if she could come ashore and see some sick people. Myra did, and realized the patients were suffering mostly from malnutrition.

At Daniel's Harbour, the man who rowed the dory out to the *Home* to greet Myra was George Moss, the community's school teacher. Myra was to stay with him and his family. They provided her with room and board as well as a place to set up a clinic and a makeshift waiting room – the kitchen. From this very basic facility, Myra faced a daunting task.

The 200 miles of rugged coast in her district was marked by an unpredictable climate and included dozens of communities. The villages were isolated and only reachable by boat, dog team, horse and, if those weren't options because of weather or availability, foot. The fact that people eked out an existence from both the earth and the ocean would add to Myra's workload. People would come to her after they cut had themselves with an axe or lodged a fish hook in their hands.

"She met a kindly people who needed her," her son Trevor says of his mother's first impressions of the town. "She never complained, but rolled up her sleeves and went to work."

Despite the absence of a communication system and the challenges of travel on the Northern Peninsula in the early 1920s, people flocked to Myra to receive medical attention for all sorts of ailments and injuries. For many, it was their first time getting any kind of treatment outside of a household remedy. And if someone was sick and couldn't reach "Nurse" – as the people fondly called Myra from the get-go – she would go to them. She went regardless of the weather, distance, her personal plans or how she was feeling herself. The patient took priority over everything.

It was her duty – to the people and the British Empire.

In August, just months after her arrival, Myra met a man named Angus Bennett as she was delivering his mother's tenth and final child. Their chance encounter was the birth of something unexpected, a relationship that would blossom and lead to marriage. Myra and the merchant marine-turned entrepreneur exchanged vows that following January, even though it was against the rules of her contract with the Outport Nursing Scheme.

While she wasn't supposed to get married while serving, by all accounts she was fortunate to find Angus. A provider and a compassionate man, he started working at the age of nine and didn't attend school after Grade 3. As a youth, he acquired survival skills in the wilds on back of Daniel's Harbour and gained self-assurance that no matter what came at him in life, he was going to make a living off the land. He took that confidence to sea with him in 1913 at age

For Myra (third from right in uniform), nursing took priority over everything. She is pictured with a group of women in Daniel's Harbour.

16 and stayed there until 1920. Angus's strength and support would play a major part in Myra's role as the region's nurse.

The Christmas after they married, the couple moved into the two-story house Angus had been building in the community. Myra made it the base of her services. And as they had at George Moss's residence, people started knocking on the door seeking attention for all sorts of medical problems at all hours of the day and night. Quite often, depending on the injury, sickness or procedure, the patient would stay at the Bennett home until they were ready and able to leave.

Despite the fact that she was putting down permanent roots in the community, Myra still made nursing her number one priority. She never relented in her willingness to travel to a patient who was 50, 100 or more miles away. Nurse continued to drop whatever she was doing to attend to patients – whether she was entertaining visitors, sleeping or tending to her regular chores, like her hens or preserves.

She would excuse herself from company and say, "I'm sorry, I just have this to do," and then take the patient into a room to extract a tooth, look at the dressing on a wound, or pull out a fish hook. She would do it in a matter-of-fact way and people – whether the patients, her guests and of course her family – came to expect it.

With her never-say-no approach and constant availability, it didn't take long before Nurse had endeared herself to the people of the area. Everyone knew she would always do the best she could in any situation and given any set of circumstances. Being alone, with no instant communication, she was forced to think quick and make decisions as she went. She was level-headed and common sense was a hallmark of her nursing. She would only treat what she felt qualified to do and would never attempt anything foolhardy. People didn't go to the hospital in those days, and if Myra felt someone required a major operation or that she couldn't treat them, she would try to send them to the nearest physician. The only hospitals were in St. Anthony and St. John's, which Trevor says may as well have been on the moon.

For the first few years, the Bennett's kitchen also served as a surgery and consultation room. Teeth were usually pulled at the kitchen table using the forceps she had brought with her from England. Bigger procedures were done privately, in a bedroom or the great room. In the early 1940s, Angus built a room on the house that would be known as "the surgery."

Myra would travel by boat, dog team, and house and sleigh. If conditions didn't allow her to use one of those methods of transportation, she walked. At times, she would walk 10 or more miles to see a patient and, according to legend, was so physically fit she would occasionally get off a dogsled and run alongside the animals. Rough seas, large snowdrifts, high winds, heavy rains – none of these stopped the dedicated and determined nurse.

The terrain was rugged in the summer and the snow was often deep in the winter. Bridges across rivers were non-existent. Myra would wade across smaller ones and cross the bigger rivers in a small boat that could be pulled from the water. She would never travel to a call alone. There was always a person willing to help carry her bag or offer a ride in a boat. And when the ever-resourceful Myra arrived at a community to attend to a patient, she would make the most of the trek by holding a clinic, making it easier for patients to come to her with their aches, pains, and ailments.

Despite such continued commitment to the people of the Northern Peninsula, and the quality of care she provided, the government of Newfoundland didn't renew her contract when it expired in 1923. Unselfishly – and something that seems unfathomable today – she continued nursing with the same sense of duty and commitment to care. She did so without pay for about 10 years, with a lot of financial and physical backing from Angus. With no access to medications or authority to send people to hospital, she would purchase drugs through her husband's business and continue to hospitalize people in her home. Besides funding health care for people in the region, Angus continued to help her travel to people in need and would do things around the house to help comfort patients. Myra never asked the people for money or thought about collecting it from them. It was no good to go after them for something they didn't have. Nurse's only payment during those 10 years was the fish or vegetables she would receive from grateful patients.

A man from Cow Head was so appreciative he even made her a table. He was a carpenter who had a hand that was badly infected. It was giving him so much pain he walked 30 miles to Daniel's Harbour. Myra ended up amputating one of his fingers and he stayed with the Bennett's for two weeks as he recovered. When he was well enough to return home, he felt indebted and asked the nurse how he could repay her. In her quick and resourceful way, Myra replied that maybe when his hand healed he could make her a better table than the one she had. Rufus

Guinchard, a Daniel's Harbour fiddler who would later receive the Order of Canada, had a homemade lathe for making table and chair legs. The carpenter went to Guinchard and asked him to make four table legs. He then placed those legs on his hand sled and towed them back to Cow Head by foot. He didn't wait for his hand to completely heal and before long had made a table. He put it on his sled and pulled it back to Daniel's Harbour. It was placed in the Bennetts' house, where it would be the site of numerous procedures, conversations and mug-ups in the decades that followed.

Myra finally started getting paid again in 1934, when the Commission of Government was formed in Newfoundland and, as a priority, wanted to address the serious lack of health services offered people, particular those in rural regions. Myra was earning a lot less than when she arrived – about $250 a year – but she took it. She now had access to drugs and medical supplies. Perhaps even more importantly, though, she now had a position of authority, and a stronger voice to lobby government. She used it persistently, informing decision makers about the need for more medical services in the region. She wanted a hospital or even a doctor. She badgered the authorities continuously and the powers-that-be eventually listened. In

> Unselfishly – and something that seems unfathomable today – she continued nursing with the same sense of duty and commitment to care. She did so without pay for about 10 years.

the late 1930s, two cottage hospitals were built in her district. One was up the coast in Port Saunders: the other was down the shore at Norris Point. There would be no more battling the elements to get patients to her kitchen for care. She would now be helping get them into a proper facility.

To no one's surprise, very quickly after her arrival and in the decades that followed, locals developed a lot of faith in Myra. They felt she could move mountains. Her to-the-point personality and sense of humour, which put patients at ease, helped endear her to the people she served. If there was tension, she could easily break it.

For example, she kept a tooth belonging to her grandson Jim in a little box and used it to help put adult patients in their place. She had pulled the tooth out of Jim's mouth when he was four and, because she thought the roots had dissolved, didn't use anaesthetic. But the roots were still very much present. Jim endured a lot of pain and Myra felt a lot of regret. And for the next 20 years or so, if she had trouble with an adult, particularly a grown man, she would pull out the box and show them the size of the tooth she had pulled out of her four-year-old grandson without deadening his gums.

> People who witnessed Myra in action as a midwife were amazed how little commotion there was as she helped women through labour. She would remain level-headed and the scene would be far more tranquil than a hospital setting.

Jim's tooth was one of more than 5,000 Myra pulled – even though she had no formal training in dentistry.

Rotting teeth – and the painful effects of it – were perhaps the most common condition Myra treated. People would show up at her door, their teeth would be the abscessed and their pain unbearable Using glass syringes she sterilized in a little dipper on the stove, Myra would deaden the area and yank out the teeth using her forceps. She would take out bottom teeth first, and there was good reason. If the top ones were extracted first, she would joke, the bottom would get bloody, making a mess and increasing the possibility of her taking the wrong tooth.

Myra, with her legendary strong wrist, continued pulling teeth long after she retired in 1953. She was actually in her early 90s when she extracted the last one in 1982, much to the horror of her family who feared she would break someone's jaw and questioned why people would still go to her at that age. But even when visiting a dentist was finally an option for residents of the Northern Peninsula, the fact that people opted to visit Myra at 90-plus for

---

STEVE BARTLETT

Myra (shown early one morning after a "baby case," according to an inscription on the photo) delivered more than 700 children.

dentistry and have her perform dental work was a true testament to their faith in her.

While painful, rotting teeth was only a minor problem. Myra helped ease the aches and halt the hurting for countless other patients, whether they had broken a limb or were sick with disease. A good many were pregnant women. During her dedicated service, she often used the midwifery skills she had honed in London during the war years. She eventually delivered more than 700 babies. The first was named Hilda White. Myra helped bring her into the world at Port Saunders in July 1921, about two months after she'd arrived in Daniel's Harbour.

People who witnessed Myra in action as a midwife were amazed at how little commotion there was as she helped women through labour. She would remain level-headed and the scene would be far more tranquil than in a hospital setting. The patient would quietly lie in her own bed. Myra would talk the mom-to-be through the contractions and the arrival. She believed in giving the expectant mother plenty of time when birthing the child. Once the baby started to arrive, she would skilfully and quickly deliver it using her forceps. There was usually little sign of blood as the child was born.

Undoubtedly, one of Myra's most special deliveries was when she delivered one of her grandsons after Christmas dinner in 1956. Fittingly, the boy was named Noel.

Years before that, Myra had come to realize that she couldn't be everywhere and, during the first six months of 1936, she took it upon herself to train a group of six area women in midwifery. She lectured them in her kitchen and took them, two at a time, to a delivery, where they would assist and gain hands-on experience. Myra even gave the women exams. She sent the finished tests to St. John's and each of her students became certified midwives.

Myra also wanted to bring her own babies into the world. She was determined to have a family and Trevor says she made that fact quite clear to his father. "She was so determined I think she told him one time that if you don't allow me to have children, I'll leave you," he laughs. "She wasn't going to be growing old without a family. She was 31 when she came and time was running out." Myra had three children. Grace was born August 27, 1923, just over two years after Myra and Angus met. Trevor came along three years later on September 3, 1926. Barbara arrived on June 24, 1930. With no midwife to assist her, Myra went to Curling to have Dr. Fisher deliver Grace. She remained home to give birth to Trevor, with a Nurse Walsh coming to relieve her and be with her at time of delivery. For Barbara, Myra again went to Dr. Fisher in Curling.

There was too much snow and too little frost for the horse to take the land route. So they rigged up a bed to a sleigh and set out over the ocean on drift ice by foot.

Perhaps the most celebrated story of Myra's years of service stemmed from an emergency situation in February 1926 when, after doing all she could, she went through a trying ordeal to get a patient to Woody Point to see the doctor. The patient was her brother-in-law, Alec. While sawing logs at a remote woods camp around dusk, he slipped and accidentally ran a rotating saw – and its razor-sharp blade – through his ankle. It almost ripped completely through, and his foot was within an inch of being severed. Some men working with him quickly and wisely elevated the leg to slow the loss of blood. Others raced from the sawmill site to fetch Myra, who was about five miles away in Daniel's Harbour. But because of the distance, the time of day, and the month of the year, reaching her was a challenge and it took a while.

STEVE BARTLETT

The men rapped on her door some time between eight and nine o'clock that night. Because of the time that had passed since the accident, Myra had to get to the sawmill as fast as possible. They immediately set out for the camp with Kit, Angus's horse. Reaching the site hours later, she rolled Alec in blankets, laid him on a wood sleigh, and had the horse pull him back to Daniel's Harbour.

Once there, Myra enlisted Dorcus Moss, a jewel of a neighbour the nurse always called on for help. Moss tried freezing Alec's leg with snow, while the nurse cleaned the wound and the debris left by his sealskin boots and woolen socks. After tucking a severely torn Achilles tendon between the skin and removing pieces of bone, Myra then sewed the foot back on the leg using silkworm gut sutures and a curved needle. It took about 30 stitches. Saving the foot wasn't her mission. She simply wanted to secure it so Alec could be transported over rugged ground and ice-filled waters to meet a doctor in Bonne Bay, roughly 60 miles south of Daniel's Harbour.

The next morning, Myra telegraphed the physician, who was stationed in Deer Lake and would do clinics in Bonne Bay. Upon hearing a description of the injury, he said it sounded like Alec would require an amputation. The doctor suggested she bring the man to Bonne Bay if possible. There was too much snow and too little frost for the horse to take the land route. So they rigged up a bed to a sleigh and set out over the ocean on drift ice by foot. Word of the medieval medivac spread down the coast through telegraph operators. When the party reached Parson's Pond that first day, a group of men were waiting with ropes and they pulled the sleigh carrying Alec up a hill to the house owned by the community's telegraph operator. They stayed the night there, with Alec sleeping on a feather bed and Myra able to get some rest as the telegraph operator watched over the patient. They left early the next morning and slowly made it to Sally's Cove, where they were taken in by another waiting family.

On the third day, they went across the ice in Bonne Bay and finally arrived at Woody Point. The doctor examined Alec. To everyone's surprise, he suggested leaving the wound alone and letting it heal. Remarkably, Myra – with her super stitching and dogged determination to reach Bonne Bay – had the saved the foot. (Amazingly, the nurse was two months pregnant with son Trevor at the time.) Although the accident left Alec with a slight limp, he worked the rest of his life and lived to 90.

There were numerous occasions when Myra enlisted other people to help care for a patient. Another example came during her treatment of a woman with toxic eclampsia – a condition that occurs during or after pregnancy. After Myra had travelled over a stormy sea at night to reach the patient, she organized people to carry out an assortment of tasks. Among the duties were bringing buckets of water from the well to the house, collecting wood to keep a fire going and the patient warm, and keeping the kettle boiled. She even got a clergyman to help her conduct a lengthy rectal irrigation.

On another occasion, she was in Cow Head treating a girl and needed medication that was back in Daniel's Harbour, which was over 50 kilometres away. One man ran with it from Daniel's Harbour to Portland Creek. Another hoofed the remedy from there to Parson's Pond. And the sick girl's brother – who had earlier run from Cow Head to Daniel's Harbour to fetch the nurse – legged it from Parson's Pond to Myra and the waiting patient in Cow Head. They weren't running on roads, but over stumps and boulders, through the woods, and across river – for much of the time in the dark of night.

Obviously, because of the challenges involved and the very nature of the work, not all of the endings were happy. Myra wasn't always able to reach the sick on time and sometimes illnesses were incurable or injuries too severe. Still, she endeavoured to give every patient the very best treatment possible. Turning them away just wasn't an option, neither was giving up. Regardless of the challenge or situation she faced, Myra didn't gripe or whine.

"There was one thing that always impressed me about Myra," says Mildred Bennett, Trevor's wife and a woman who nursed alongside Myra. "She never got upset if things went wrong. If she

Myra receiving her honourary degree from Memorial University in 1974.

got disappointed, she never showed it...If it were me, I would probably moan and complain...but never her. That's the way it was. This is what impressed me most of all. She would always say there is a reason for everything."

Another of Myra's challenges, almost from the moment she arrived at Daniel's Harbour, was educating the people in the region about health issues and diseases such as tuberculosis. She would tell people the deadly lung disease illness was contagious and they would disagree, telling stories about people who didn't catch it from family or friends who had come down with the illness.

Myra "retired" in 1953 (the same year she and a friend took a trip around the world by boat, steaming to places such as Africa and India). Even though she was off the payroll, for the next 30 years, she continued to perform many of the nursing tasks she had carried out since arriving more than three decades earlier.

Outside of the 200 miles she served, Myra's undying commitment and tireless effort on the Northern Peninsula went unnoticed for decades. But that all seemed to change in the early 1970s. In 1974, prolific Canadian writer H. Gordon Green

Nurse Bennett Heritage House is now a provincial historic site and museum.

penned a biography about Myra entitled, *Don't Have Your Baby in the Dory.* She was also featured in *Reader's Digest* and on various CBC-TV programs. And *The Evening Telegram* dubbed her "The Florence Nightingale of the North."

She received the Order of Canada from Governor General Jules Leger in 1974, the same year she was bestowed an honourary Doctor of Science degree from Memorial University. She was also awarded a medallion coinciding with King George V's jubilee, a coronation medal from Queen Elizabeth, and was made an honourary member of the Association of Registered Nurses of Newfoundland.

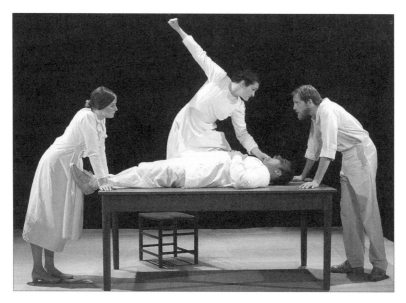

A scene from *Tempting Providence*, a play based on Myra Bennett's life that has been staged across Canada and around the world.

Although he never officially received such recognition from universities or dignitaries, Angus Bennett deserves a lot of credit for helping Myra achieve what she did. He is the unsung hero in the nursing legacy. Throughout the years, he assisted his wife – and ultimately the people of the region – in so many ways. He would share his muscle and wherewithal as well as his food, horse, boat, and anything else he had. Angus gave tirelessly and never complained. He would shrink into the background unless Myra needed him. "Mom would not have been able to provide the service she did, under such extremely difficult circumstances without a man like my father," says Trevor. "His door was open to all who came his way for a meal, a place to sleep or for medical attention."

The nurse would be gracious about receiving such honours, but she was not one to rest on her laurels or stand on ceremony. She never thought she was doing anything out of the ordinary. What she had done for all those years was just part of a day's work.

Myra passed away in Daniel's Harbour in late April 1990, less than a month after she reached the century mark. Her home and hospice, Bennett House, has since been made into a museum and provincial historic site. It is now a popular destination with those exploring Route 430, the highway that went through Daniel's Harbour a few years after Myra retired.

As well, the story of Myra's dedication and commitment to the people she served continues to be told around the world. She is the subject of *Tempting Providence*, a hugely successful play that has been staged as far away as the United Kingdom and Australia since its 2002 premiere at the Gros Morne Theatre Festival in Cow Head.

Robert Chafe, the talented playwright behind the show, says he was initially struck by the volume of Myra's work – the 700 births and 5,000 teeth – but as he dug deeper, what amazed him was that Myra came here for two years only, but after one year was married and had committed her life to staying.

> "I think she was just motivated by the work that she loved doing," says her son Trevor.

That's also what intrigues Myra's grandson Jim (the guy whose tooth was pulled without anaesthesia at four). Of all the amazing stories and legends attributed to his grandmother, he says the fact she settled in a place with next to no conveniences is most incredible. "For her to say, 'I think I'm going to marry this guy and stay here and raise a family,' that really boggles my mind more than any of this stuff that she did," he says. "For her to make a commitment and stay and raise a family, knowing what she knew about the world and where she had come from?"

But what motivated Myra to do what she did and make such sacrifices for such a long time? It certainly wasn't money, as is obvious by the decade that she basically volunteered and the many free services she provided people from the time she retired up until she was in her 90s. Myra's family thinks she was driven by a sense of duty to people and to the British Empire.

"I think she was just motivated by the work that she loved doing," says Trevor. "She always believed that everybody was born to do a decent day's work. That was her philosophy. She found the work that she really enjoyed doing and anyone in need she was always there to help them. She was a busy lady and her life was so busy, and that's what she enjoyed doing. She found her niche, helping people, and I think that motivated her right until the end."

It might be hard to imagine Myra's thoughts when she landed at Daniel's Harbour for the first time, but it's even more difficult to think about how the people of her region would have fared had she not come and made such an exceptional and loving commitment.

TOMMY SEXTON

IF PEOPLE COME into the world with a distinct purpose, Tommy Sexton arrived to entertain. Born July 3, 1957, he started performing for people at age two, perhaps even a few months before turning the tender age usually associated with being terrible. Under the watch of his older sister Edwina, Tommy the talented toddler would travel Gower Street, where the Sextons lived in the late 1950s and early sixties, and break into song for the older people of the downtown St. John's neighbourhood. "Now granted they'd probably give him a quarter," chuckles his mother Sara, who would accompany the boy on some of the musical missions. "I never asked him that, but Edwina would come back to me and say, 'Tom sang and they loved him.'"

The older folks in the row housing of Gower Street were the first audiences to love Tommy, but they would hardly be the last. In the years and decades that followed, he would become one of

Tommy had the lead role in *Oliver!* in his early teens. During the show's run at the St. John's Arts and Culture Centre, he also acted as the character in a speak-off, delighting the audience and the judges.

Newfoundland's most famous sons, a legend of Canadian comedy and an icon for the nation's gay community.

Tommy's love of performing was arguably passed down from Sara. At age five or six, she was doing dialogues on stage during variety shows staged by the nuns in St. Mary's, a small community on Newfoundland's Avalon Peninsula. "I loved it," she says. "There was nothing like it in my life to compare with it...when you sing a song or say a recitation and people would clap." Sara's brothers were also excellent storytellers, with an ability to spin tales that made people laugh until they cried. Whenever her siblings stopped by the Sexton house on Gower, Tommy would feed off them. And he would sing to them too, sometimes in French. "And he was loving it," Sara says.

Tommy was the fifth of the nine children that Sara and her husband Edward would have. He was always eccentric and hyperactive as a boy. He took singing lessons and, in Grade 2, played Alice when St. Bonaventure's College – or St. Bon's, as the all-boys Catholic school was commonly called – staged *Alice in Wonderland*. Tommy also sang at Kiwanis Music Festivals in St. John's and won awards for his soprano voice. It soon became quite obvious that he was fascinated with the stage. He started hanging out at the St. John's Arts and Culture Centre, spending every minute he could there.

Tommy got involved with Sylvia Wigh's Young People's Theatre when he was about twelve. He would often drag a couple of his brothers along, much against their will, to back him up. Wigh, who would produce shows involving dozens of young people, sensed something special in Tommy and gave him the lead in *Oliver!*, the musical adaptation of Charles Dickens' classic novel *Oliver Twist*. Tommy soared in the role of the naïve orphan, playing to packed houses and earning loud ovations. Sara considers Oliver to be the role that really highlighted Tommy's talent and potential. "That was like a signpost for him," she says. "That told him that he could do it." She remembers being approached one night during the show's run by Lord Stephen Taylor, then president of Memorial University. A former British member of Parliament who was named to the House of Lords, he had seen an impressive production of *Oliver!* in London, where the musical was based and first produced. But Taylor told Sara that Tommy was better in the role than the boy who performed the lead across the pond. "I said, 'That's marvelous,' because he would be one to say the London fella was better, but he didn't," Sara recalls. "He said, 'Not nearly as good as Tommy,' so from then on I did anything I could to help." That meant encouraging and supporting her aspiring actor in any way possible. "Money was scarce," she says. "We had a big crowd. We couldn't afford to do the things for him that I would like to do for him. I would like to have been able to send him to dancing school."

At the same time as he was garnering rave reviews in *Oliver!*, Tommy was involved in a speak-off at Mary Queen of Peace, the Roman Catholic church not far from where the Sextons now lived in St. John's East End. His father, who was known as Ned, picked him up at the Arts and Culture Centre and brought him to the speak-off dressed as Oliver. Tommy gave his speech in character and he also sang. After receiving thunderous applause, a priest, Father Connolly, asked the boy what he hoped to do when he grew up. Tommy replied that he wanted to be an actor and, from that point on, he was.

Tommy's parents were both educators. Sara taught primary at the Mount Cashel orphanage and later at St. Bonaventure's College. Ned was a high school teacher and later became a school supervisor. He also tutored and taught night classes to earn some extra money to support his large family. Despite the pedigree and the fact he did extremely well in school without studying much, Tommy didn't place a lot of emphasis on education, especially after *Oliver!* He wanted to spend his time on stage, not sitting behind a classroom desk learning about trigonometry or trajectories. His parents emphasized and preached how important education would be for whatever he planned to do – even acting. But they had little luck convincing or telling him to take school seriously, especially after he got involved with the Newfoundland Traveling Theatre Company, a troupe founded by Dudley Cox and David Weiser that toured the island's outports. "When he got a touch of being on the road," Sara recalls, "he hardly wanted to finish Grade Eleven and, of course, his father was seeing stars."

But Tommy was seeing different kinds of stars – future stars. The cast of the first play he did with the traveling company included a group of talented young actors he would work closely with in the years that followed: Andy Jones, Bob Joy, Diane Olsen and Mary Walsh. The play was *See How They Run*, a 1940s British farce by Philip King that gets its title from the nursery rhyme "Three Blind Mice." Tommy toured with that show from the latter part of June to the end of July 1972. In August, he went back on the road with the company as it toured *Pool's Paradise*, another Philip King farce. His cast mates were Olsen, Walsh and Greg Malone, an actor Tommy would later collaborate with most. "We met then and got to be good friends," Malone says. "When Tommy is your friend, you don't lose him." Sara figures the traveling company's plays were beyond the teenaged Tommy's age level, but he thought otherwise. She says he did his best at whatever role he accepted, and at that time, Wigh was a big encouragement.

Tommy enjoyed his experience with the traveling troupe so much that he signed on for a second summer in '73. The play was *Starrigan*, and besides Tommy and Olsen, the cast included Cathy Jones, yet another actress who would play a big role in Tommy's future. Signing on for another tour was troubling for his parents. Not because they were necessarily against him touring, but because the company was hitting the road before the school year ended. They urged Tommy to write his provincial exams, and he promised to do so in Grand Falls, the central Newfoundland town where the tour would be when the tests were administered. But when Tommy called a few days after the exams were given and his mother asked if he had taken the tests, she didn't get the answer she was anticipating. "No Mom, it never crossed my mind," she recalls Tommy saying. It was disappointing and frustrating at the time, but recounting the story now makes Sara laugh. She concedes that education just wasn't a priority for him, that "acting and singing and dancing was Tom's life."

In fact, Tommy never ever wrote another exam, again to his teacher parents' utter dismay. Instead, after finishing up *Starrigan*, he dropped a bombshell on the Sextons by heading to Toronto to pursue his goal. Accompanied by Olsen, he left with no money and no idea where he was going to stay or how he was going to eat. Ned, who was constantly at odds with Tommy, was so furious he even threatened to call the Royal Canadian Mounted Police to ask them to bring his son home. Looking back, Malone says, there was no stopping Tommy, he was just that intense about following his dream. "I don't know many fifteen-year-olds, especially at that time in the early '70s, with that amount of gumption," Malone says. "That required a lot of nerve really."

In Toronto, Tommy was hired to perform in schools with a children's show called *Fables*. After getting an agent, he landed a role in a TV series called *Police Surgeon*. It followed the adventures of a former country doctor that had joined a big city police force as its staff surgeon. The series ran Saturday nights on CTV. Although it was described as "sub sub par" by *Variety* magazine, it attracted some impressive guest stars, including *Star Trek's* William Shatner and Leslie Nielsen, who later starred in *Police Squad* and *Naked Gun* fame.

That first year in Toronto, Tommy and Olsen also auditioned for a part in a show being staged by Theatre Passe Muraille, a cutting-edge company now considered Canada's first alternative theatre group. Apparently the Newfoundlanders didn't land a part because of their St. John's brogue, but they made such an impression on the troupe's artistic director that he gave them $300 to write a script. They started penning the play and enlisted Cathy Jones and Paul Sametz – their roommates at the time – to help write it. They also asked Malone, then working as an actor in Toronto, to get involved. "I resisted as long as I could, but Tommy was very persuasive," he remembers. "I finally had to go over and sit down and start in on [it]. I ended up directing it. We didn't have very many actors. I ended up acting in it too." Mary

Walsh, who at the time was also a roommate and a theatre student at Ryerson, was soon on board too. The result: *Cod On A Stick*, a series of sketches and songs about how Mainlanders viewed Newfoundlanders. The show was in line with the revue tradition – music, dance and sketches mixed together – and dealt with their home province. "That play was a direct reaction, an overwhelming reaction, to the overwhelmingly negative stereotype that we encountered in Toronto in the 1970s and this was our cultural reaction to that," Malone later recalled. "We were the Newfie joke, a position we shared with Polacks and the Irish...it was the time of these wonderful humourous jokes about Polacks and the stupid lazy Newfs, and of course, our bog-trodding brethren from the Auld Sod, the Irish. We all shared that distinction." Besides standing tall for Newfoundland, the play also turned out to be the birth of *CODCO*, a name conceived by Malone that was short for Cod Company.

Cod On A Stick premiered in October 1973 – just months after Sexton first landed in Toronto. It was performed in a church annex and ran roughly a half-hour, with a line-up that included Sexton, Olsen, Malone, Walsh, Jones and Sametz. The locale and duration of the show didn't keep audiences away. It was so successful, the troupe mounted it for the next three months. By February, they were performing it in St. John's, thanks to CBC Radio, which recorded it live. And that spring *CODCO* – with a few lineup changes, including the addition of Bob Joy in Sametz's original role – took it across the province. They traveled in a van the troupe purchased with grant money available because Newfoundland was celebrating the twenty-fifth anniversary of joining Canada. In August 1974, the play was filmed by the National Film Board, and for that performance, brought in another actor, Cathy Jones' brother Andy. Sara Sexton feels *Cod On A Stick* was memorable because it was so good and well put together. "It was ahead of its time," she says.

Based on the success of their inaugural play – which started putting some money in the young actors' pockets – the troupe compiled more revue-style shows over the next three years. The core line-up included Sexton, the Joneses, Olsen, Malone, Walsh, and Joy. These are the seven who would be considered *CODCO*. No topic was off limits in their shows. From development to outmigration to child abuse, they tackled touchy topics using a variety of different techniques. The actors incorporated song, dance, mime and even puppets into their collectively-written performances. They toured the works throughout Canada, and played festivals in the United States, England and Montreal, where a collection of previous materials was put together and performed as part of the 1976 Olympics. *CODCO*'s work was raw and ground-breaking. Later it would be studied and appreciated at the university level and published in a book, *The Plays of CODCO*, in 1992.

For Tommy, the motivation was simple and unchanged from his days hanging around the St. John's Arts and Culture Centre – he wanted to be on stage and to make people laugh. "He wanted that hold," Malone says. "He wanted to create that. He was a big party guy and this was the biggest party of all, the stage show." And *CODCO* shows often resulted in big bashes. Audiences would stay around to chat after the curtain went down and often a huge party would break out. Besides taking command of a stage, there were few things the openly gay Tommy enjoyed as much as a party. "He was very, very social," Malone says. "He never had to go to one party on a Saturday night. He had two or three that he would go to."

In 1975, Tommy took a break from *CODCO* to study at the Toronto Dance Theatre. He spent about a year there, but came back to St. John's because he couldn't afford it. That Tommy didn't study dance more appears to be a source of some regret for Sara Sexton, who wishes she could have afforded to keep him in the school. "He was a beautiful dancer," she says. Tommy returned to *CODCO* and stayed until the members went their separate ways the following year after producing *The Tale Ends*, which was about the history of theatre. Joy headed to the United States to pursue his career there. Olsen gave up acting. The rest of the crowd, including Tommy, just kept trying to do what they seemed to do best – entertaining.

The years after *CODCO* split saw Tommy involved in an assortment of projects, many of which included his comedic colleagues. He had a part in *The Adventures of Fautus Bidgood*, a feature film by Andy Jones and his brother Michael that started filming in 1977, but wasn't released until 1986. He also acted in a couple of plays, and two cabarets staged by a *CODCO*-esque ensemble calling itself The White Niggers of Bond Street, which also included Walsh and the Joneses. Tommy then joined Malone in a project called the Wonderful Grand Band, which had stemmed from *The Root Cellar*, a popular six-part CBC TV series that mixed music and sketches. After the short 1978 series wrapped up, the band assembled for it had stayed together and toured. Malone, one of the series' co-writers and actors, stuck around too, allowing the mix of song and satire to continue. Tommy joined him in 1980. It was a wise decision. That same year, the act landed its own TV series, *The Wonderful Grand Band*, or *WGB* for short.

While *CODCO* had given Tommy reputation and renown, being part of the *WGB* made him a Newfoundland icon. *The Wonderful Grand Band* quickly became the most popular show and entertainment act in the province. The thirty-minute television episodes mixed the zany antics of the Budgells, played by Sexton and Malone, with rock-infused traditional music from an ensemble of some of the best music makers in the province's history, including Ron Hynes and Sandy Morris. The show was not to be missed. Young girls would line-up outside the bars where they played – not to try to sneak in and see the act live, but just to get a glimpse of the band members. It was Bugdell-mania, and the members of the band were like rock stars. Tommy Sexton and Greg Malone became household names, as did some of the recurring characters they played on the show. Tommy's most memorable roles were Dickie Budgell and Nanny Hynes. Sara Sexton remembers those days fondly. She recalls pushing through the crowds at The Strand Lounge in the Avalon Mall to see the *WGB* and hear the music. She thought it was marvelous and new. "It would just draw you in," she says. Sara also has fond recollections of the first time she saw Tommy doing a sketch with the *WGB*. It was a skit about a crowded rural taxi, something she could relate to from her youth, and it still makes her laugh. "I thought I would have to be carried out I laughed so much," she chuckles, "because I had driven from St. Mary's with the taxi. No room, just get in and sit on somebody most of the time. And then, of course, the taxi would stop and let the people go [pee] in the woods. My God, when we saw them doing that." Sara says that while some might have thought the skits were making fun of Newfoundlanders, she figures they were simply traveling back in the past and showing how things were.

At its peak, the *WGB* was the most popular program ever evaluated by Canada's ratings system. It also made traditional music cool and fueled a cultural renaissance. Many of the top entertainers from the province today, from the folk band Great Big Sea to comedian Rick Mercer, were inspired by *The Wonderful Grand Band*. The show highlighted Sexton and Malone's comedic genius – and their ability to play an assortment of characters, male or female – to a wide audience. "I remember many people saying to me, 'How foolish is he at all?' " Sara Sexton recalls. "I mean foolish – I could never attach foolish to what they were doing. It was profound really." *The Wonderful Grand Band* series ran until 1983, recording more than forty shows. Cathy Jones and Mary Walsh were part of the act in the final year, when a number of episodes were shown nationally and the band toured Canada.

The *WGB* disbanded shortly after, but Tommy's star continued to rise. He and Greg were soon flat-out with a two-man show they wrote called *Too Foolish To Talk About*. "He was a great instigator like that," says Malone. "He wouldn't let any grass grow under our feet or much time lapse before we were into something else, which was great for me because I loved having someone to work with and push me." The duo criss-crossed the country with the show in 1984 and took it to TV, entering *The S&M Comic Book* in a regional CBC contest for new programs. The show won and led to three specials on the national network, each of them earning Gemini Awards, which honour the best in Canadian television. "*S &M Comic Book,* that was great," Sara says. "It gave the two of them a chance to do something worthwhile." Malone, who considered Tommy part of his family and says they were like an old married couple, remembers it being a particularly enjoyable period of their friendship. "It was hugely fun," he says. "We did so much laughing, and we were very close."

During the same period, *CODCO* – minus Joy and Olsen – reunited for a benefit, and the troupe's farcical flame rekindled. They decided to stay together, mounting a comeback show and a national tour. Salter Street Films out of Halifax approached the troupe with the idea of bringing their antics to television. Beginning in 1986, *CODCO* was part of CBC-TV Newfoundland's programming for two seasons and then added to the national line-up for five seasons. Through this series – filmed in a Halifax studio, with location shots done in St. John's – Cod Company showcased its collective ability to write satire and lampoon everything. The show's social and political edge was biting and the country's audiences were also bitten. As it had been since the early days of *Cod On A Stick,* no subject was sacred. They took aim at everything from politics to religion to sexual orientation to TV personalities, but now with quality make-up and sets to enhance the effect.

At its peak, the WGB was the most popular program ever evaluated by Canada's ratings system. It also made traditional music cool and fueled a cultural renaissance.

The *CODCO* cast quickly became known for the colourful characters they portrayed, many which involved cross-dressing. There was Jerome and Duncan (gay lawyers played by Sexton and Malone, respectively), the Friday Night Girls (Walsh and Cathy Jones' portrayal of bored and homely women with little to do) and Frank Arsenpuffin (a disgruntled talk show host played Andy Jones). The boyish Tommy's contribution to the collective, his characters and ideas for satire, came from all over. "He was inspired by everything," Malone says. "He would drag me off to see dance shows. He would say, 'No Greg, we'll have a great time making fun of this. You've got to come and see this,' just so we could write about it." People would approach the always social Tommy, Malone adds, and ask where he got his material. He would tell them to just keeping talking. "He'd go down to a gay club and come home with lines, great lines, great characters," Malone continues. "And we'd say, 'Oh God, that deserves a scene,' and we'd settle down and start writing the scene."

Tommy would often base characters on family and friends. Because the topics were often controversial, Sara says, "[I] would often say to myself, 'Dear God, I hope they don't recognize themselves.'" She would always get a queer feeling inside when new episodes aired and remembers being particularly anxious when Tommy would spoof his father or Sister Mary Moo, a character based on a nun who often visited the Sexton house. "And then she used to come in and say she saw it and loved it and all the nuns loved it. And you know who that character is, that's Mother Superior, used to be down at Mercy. She didn't recognize herself, my God." Sara, a devoutly religious woman, admits she always had a hard time accepting some of the church-based sketches and characters. "I would be bad for that," she says.

Many of the *CODCO* characters involved the actors cross-dressing. Tommy relished that. He loved costumes, wigs and makeup, and he was quite convincing when portraying a woman. Sara remembers seeing photos of a character named Crystal. "He brought home the pictures and laid them on the table and I said, 'Tom, they are gorgeous.' And I said, 'Who did they get to do Crystal? And he said, 'Now, you should know her,' and I said no." She suggested that it might be an actress or singer from Halifax. "I said, 'I give up Tom,' and he said, 'That's me, Mom.'" Sara says he was thrilled that his own mother didn't recognize him. Of all the characters he did, she figures his favourite was Nanny Hynes, a constantly blinking, hairnetted grandmother he made hugely popular in the *Wonderful Grand Band* days. "He used to say it was like my mother," Sara says. "My mother was very old fashioned."

Malone says Tommy made people love that woman, and notes he was always sensitive when portraying the young and elderly.

Because of sketches concerning homosexual issues, Sexton is often considered a pioneer. Malone says that, as far as he knows, Tommy was the first actor to be openly gay in Canada on television on any network. "We did a lot of scenes about that and we [brought] a lot of gay characters to the Canadian screen, where there had been none before and none since," he says, acknowledging that *The Kids in the Hall*, an edgy sketch comedy regularly paired with *CODCO* in the CBC line-up, also portrayed some homosexual characters. Malone remembers one sketch where he did his dead-on impersonation of the late CBC broadcaster Barbara Frum and Tommy did a woman from a fictional group called COWS, or Citizens Opposed to Weird Sex. Being part of such satire endeared Tommy to Canada's gay community. "Oh my God, they loved it," Malone says. "He was an icon to them."

Tommy, according to Malone, also played a big behind-the-scenes role within *CODCO*. He says that, whenever there were disputes or creative differences, Sexton would be the one to try and make things right. "He was a very positive guy and he was a peacemaker in the group," Malone says. "He didn't like to fight."

One event that Tommy, nor anyone else in the troupe, could fix was Andy Jones' anger over the CBC's decision in 1990 not to run, in the wake of the Mount Cashel Orphanage scandal, a sketch he had written where Roman Catholic priests talk about their sexual experiences. Jones quit the troupe in protest.

In 1992, Sexton and Malone pointed their satire at the Canadian constitutional debates of the time and produced a national television special for the CBC called *The National Doubt*. In it, they played a pair of medieval characters, a knight and his squire, who crossed Canada to see how people viewed the constitution. Also in 1992, *Buried on a Sunday*, a feature film about a small Nova Scotian community trying to become a superpower, was released, starring Tommy, Mary Walsh and Andy Jones.

The Tommy Sexton Centre is one of the actor/comedian's greatest legacies.

CODCO ended its TV run in 1993. The show was considered revolutionary by many, with some saying it changed comedy in Canada. Many Newfoundlanders valued it because it helped change perceptions about their home province and the people from it – the original goal of *Cod On A Stick*. The show picked up numerous Geminis over the years and toured across Canada, in the United States and in England. By now its members were known and loved nationally for their searing satire and colourful, but true-to-life characters. Tommy also had notoriety for another reason. He was dying from an AIDS-related condition. Word of his condition spread, and just as he had been a trailblazer in comedy and gay rights, he was now a pioneer in AIDS education and tolerance. "There is still a huge stigma attached to HIV and AIDS, and I think when Tommy came out and said that he was a homosexual and said that he was dying of AIDS, it put a human face to it," his sister, film producer Mary Sexton, told the CBC years later. "...Nanny Hynes was sick...It wasn't just some queer fellow Downtown that was sick, it was someone that we loved." Because Tommy lived so intensely and burned the candle at both ends, Malone says he had a terrible feeling that Tommy wouldn't last long once he became ill.

His hunch was right. In November 1993, as they were working on a feature film called *Adult Children of Alcoholics: The Musical*, Tommy became too sick to finish it and the project was shelved. He died weeks later on December 13th, 1993, at Malone's house with his mother lying next to him. "The darn old AIDS took him, but it wasn't his life," Sara says. "It was the death of him, but his life was worthwhile, and he died as I'd like for him to die. I lay down on the bed with him and about twenty to four in the morning he woke, and his eyes were as bright as they ever were and I said, 'Oh my God, he is getting better.' And that's the only thing that struck me, and a minute after, it struck me just as hard [that] he is dying. He went out of life very quietly and left his mark, no question about that."

That mark remains in many ways. With *CODCO*, he helped change the face of Canadian comedy. With the *WGB*, he helped make Newfoundland song and satire cool. And with AIDS, he helped others understand and cope. Tommy has been remembered formally in many ways, as in the Gemini-winning documentary his sister Mary made in 2001 called *Tommy: A Family Portrait*. There's also a triple-threat scholarship at Sir Wilfred Grenfell College's fine arts program that recognizes a theatre student who can act, dance and sing. His likeness is also part of a sculpture by Morgan MacDonald at the base of the infamous George Street, saluting the vibrant arts scene in St. John's. But the biggest, and most substantive, monument to his memory is the Tommy Sexton Centre, which provides emergency shelter, housing and support to Newfoundlanders and Labradorians living with HIV and AIDS. The $1.4 million facility opened in St. John's in 2006 and offers the kind of assistance Tommy tried to give others when he was sick. "He said I'm all right, I got money. I can take care of myself. I can get pills. I can get treatment," Malone recalls. "But other people, he said, they didn't even have places to live. He did some work in Halifax along those lines, trying to help people who were not in such fortunate circumstances as he was." Sara thinks the centre is what Tom, as a gay man, would have wanted more than anything. What he did to raise AIDS awareness, she suggests, is one of her son's greatest achievements of all.

Malone says it's hard to say what Tommy's greatest legacy might be. He lauds Sexton's talent, joy of performing and brilliant characters, but says there are two things he remembers most. One is Tommy's kindness and loving disposition. "It would always shine forth in the end. He never liked to leave things in a negative way," Malone says. "He wasn't too proud to apologize and make things right. And you couldn't resist that ultimately, even if you were mad at him." The other thing he recalls is Tommy's devotion to justice. Sexton, he says, was always kind to people who were impoverished, going through difficult times or being discriminated against. "He was always lending a helping hand to people, and in our work, he was always very devoted to gay rights, and doing theatre about gay rights and gay characters." Had Tommy lived longer, Malone thinks he would have accomplished more in TV, theatre and film. "I'm sure he would have kept dazzling people. He would have been well known today if he had kept going."

It was only after Tommy died, Sara admits, that she and Ned really learned how successful their son had been and how many people he had touched. The family received letters and correspondence from friends and fans following his death. The notes stated what Tommy had meant to them. Sara recalls volunteering with her husband at a cancer hostel after Tommy passed and being approached by a deeply-depressed woman who was battling the disease. The patient told the Sextons that Tommy gave her needed laughter. "She said, 'I cried and cried when he died because he had left so much, he had done so much, to lift our hearts,'" Sara says. "She was so thankful for his life and it certainly told us a lot. It told his father a lot...that it is a very important thing." Even the night before she was interviewed for this book, in the summer of 2008, a woman approached Sara with thoughts on Tommy. "She said, 'God, I loved Tom.' She said he

Tommy Sexton

was in my heart and he will never go away... So you know he has put himself into people's hearts, and I think to me that is the most important thing."

Sara says her son was continuously striving to be the best he could. She always thinks back to something he said to her just before he passed away. "He said to me, 'I didn't do too bad, Mom. I did all right.' I said, 'You did wonderful, Tom.'"

W.J. HERDER

TOWARDS THE LATTER part of the 1870s, people told William James Herder that a daily newspaper would never last in St. John's, then a city of 30,000. But the twenty-nine-year-old printer wasn't phased by the naysayers. Almost 130 years later, his dream, *The Evening Telegram*, is the oldest continuous daily newspaper in Newfoundland and Labrador. Over its lengthy existence, the paper – now known as *The Telegram* – has informed its readers about some of the biggest events in the history of Newfoundland as a colony, as a self-governing dominion, and as a Canadian province. From the Great Fire of 1892 to the Newfoundland Regiment's near decimation at Beaumont Hamel in 1916 to the province's joining Canada in 1949, *The Evening Telegram* has documented events of significance to the island (although coverage of the fire was a little delayed for reasons explained). If it wasn't for Herder's drive and integrity in the publication's early days, the paper would never have survived and played its vital role in delivering the news.

Herder was born in Old Perlican, Trinity Bay, on October 6, 1849, to Sarah Woodland and John Herder. Three years later, after his father died in a hunting accident, Sarah, W.J. and the family's other son, George, moved to St. John's. W.J. attended Methodist Academy and, at fourteen, left school to apprentice as a printer with a biweekly paper called *Courier*. The publication's owner, William Beck, sold it to the Woods brothers, and under Joseph Woods, Herder was promoted to foreman of the business, which besides publishing the newspaper also did job printing. When the Woods hit financial turmoil in 1877, they stopped publishing *Courier*, but continued taking on print work. Two years later, with sixteen years of experience behind him, Herder was successful in his bid to buy the business.

He decided to use the equipment, which was old, to start a daily paper. It was a media venture that had not previously succeeded in Newfoundland. The time, however, must have felt right for the ambitious master printer. The economic prospects for the island looked bright. The fishery was peaking, some mining operations were being encouraged, and there was a lot of talk about establishing a railway. Even though the printed word was the main method of communicating at the time, many skeptics said a daily couldn't and wouldn't work. Still, Herder proceeded and launched *The Evening Telegram*. "It was a tremendous, courageous thing to take on," Newfoundland historian Maudie Whalen said in a 2005 article on Herder published in *The Independent*, a now defunct weekly. "It was a very iffy proposition. In fact, it was called "Herder's folly," because there were so many papers around at the time....But he had the courage to do it, he stuck it out and, basically, he's still around while others have gone by the wayside."

Volume 1, Number 1, of *The Evening Telegram* was published on April 3, 1879, with a staff of six that included Herder as publisher, Alexander Parsons as editor, and Robert Mercer as pressman. Parsons, a Harbour Grace native who had worked in printing at both St. John's and Boston, wrote the copy and typeset it. Mercer used a hand press to produce the less than 500 copies of the four-page first edition. In terms of length and width, the paper was a little more than one-quarter the size of a modern-day broadsheet. A copy sold for a cent – it was the first Newfoundland paper to ask such a price – and an annual subscription cost $3.20 (although many thought the endeavour wouldn't survive a year).

The front page of the first edition included wire copy from *The Halifax Telegraph*, world news, a few local items and ads. When readers turned the page, they got commentary on page two and advertising on page three. There was a mix of content on page four. It included more local news, serial fiction, poetry and advertising. "*The Telegram*, from the outset, had a lot of eye-appeal," Michael Harrington wrote in *The Atlantic Advocate* in 1979, 100 years after Herder rolled the presses. "The staff used a variety of type; in fact no less than twenty-nine type faces had appeared as early as July 1879." Not everyone shares the same opinion about the paper's early attractiveness. Whelan told *The Independent* the inaugural editions were "not that good looking, not so interesting to look at."

The Evening Telegram was attractive to people at the time though. The paper was well received, but faced stiff competition in catching the attention of people who lived in St. John's. At the time, eight other newspapers were being published in the city. One was three times a week and the other seven were twice a week. Herder and his crew plodded on, and in the early editions, promoted themselves as much as possible. The April 8, 1879 paper – issue number five – included a note "To Business Men." It stated they "would do well to advertise their Goods, &c., in *The Evening Telegram*. We now circulate, in this city alone, nearly six hundred copies." The following day, on page two, there was an anecdote about a "languid-looking man" who had come into the paper's office. "In answer to our enquiry as to the cause of his weakness, he informed us that he had walked three miles to

An early copy of The Evening Telegram. The paper was almost two months old when this edition hit the streets.

obtain a copy of our paper. We need say no more. This is sufficient evidence of the estimation in which *The Evening Telegram* is held." Whatever Herder and his staff were doing – whether it concerned their product, the promotion, or a combination – it worked. Within two weeks, the paper had doubled in size to eight pages. Three months after its launch, the determined Herder purchased a new press that was capable of printing 1,000 copies per day.

By May 1880, 2,000 copies of *The Evening Telegram* were being published from Monday to Saturday. As circulation climbed, more staff were hired and new equipment was added. The publication moved from the old *Courier* offices on Duckworth Street to Gregory's Lane, which connected Duckworth Street and Water Street. A new, cutting edge press capable of producing 1,800 papers an hour was put in place at the new location. The publication also continued to increase the size of its news staff. In a *Telegram* column about Herder in 1998, archivist Bert Riggs said the extra reporters boosted local coverage and reduced the reliance on the international news fed from other publications. The paper also introduced illustrations, perhaps as a Christmas gift to readers. The first drawing appeared Dec. 24, 1881. (Photographs were introduced years later, and in 1935, the first staff photographer was hired. His name was Albert Young.)

Herder wed a St. John's girl named Elizabeth Barnes on April 29, 1882. Shortly after the nuptials, his publication accidentally took on a new look. A shipment of pink paper addressed to the *Toronto Telegram* – which was also known as *The Evening Telegram* – arrived in St. John's instead. Forced to use it because he had no other newsprint, Herder and his presses rolled with it. The pink prompted a competing publisher to claim that *The Evening Telegram* blushed when Herder got married. The colour, though, was apparently popular with readers, and Herder continued publishing with it. Asked for an explanation, he replied it was "because all the rest are white." The paper was printed in pink until February 7, 1942 – almost sixty years later – and it was only stopped because shipments were cut off by World War II.

The Great Fire of 1892 flattened the eastern side of St. John's, leaving thousands homeless and burning numerous businesses to the ground. *The Evening Telegram* was among them, however, within seven weeks, it was back on the streets.

Over its first decade or so, *The Evening Telegram* continued growing, outlasting competitors and silencing the skeptics. But the paper's progress was interrupted on July 8, 1892, when fire broke out in a stable on Freshwater Road and eventually destroyed the eastern side of St. John's. The Great Fire of 1892, as it was called, was the worst blaze in the city's history. The downtown area, which included *The Evening Telegram* building, was in ruins. Of nearby Water Street, one eyewitness said both sides were "swept with the besom of destruction." It was estimated that as many as 12,000 people were left homeless. Numerous businesses found themselves burned to the ground down. Herder, however, didn't only lose his building: he also lost a new press that was sitting at dockside waiting to be transported to the paper's offices.

STEVE BARTLETT

The first edition of *The Evening Telegram* after the Great Fire of 1892. The post-blaze issue hit the streets Sept. 1, 1892.

The publisher had insurance, but only enough to cover a fraction of his losses. Banks wouldn't give him a loan to rebuild. He was turned down either because of the money required by other businesses also trying to recover from the devastation or because he was seen as a risk, according to a story in *The Evening Telegram* on the fiftieth anniversary of his death. But Herder was determined to get his presses going again. Charles Robert Ayre, a prominent St. John's businessman who operated Ayre and Sons, stepped in and backed Herder. On September 1, 1892 – about seven weeks after the Great Fire – *The Evening Telegram* was back on the streets. Its Water Street interim location was later described by a rival newspaper, in admiration of Herder's perseverance, as a shed.

Unlike today, during that period, advertising was common on the front page of *The Evening Telegram*. An ad for Ayre and Sons was front and centre in the first post-fire issue. It read – fittingly summing up the mood of many businesses that had been razed – "Fire can Destroy, but Labour can Restore." The four-page issue featured a lengthy article about the fire on page two and commentary/promotion on page four. "*The Evening Telegram* rising Phoenix-like from the ashes, enters a new career of daily ministration," the editorial read. "With fresh vigour, and equipped with the modern and most approved appliances of the printer's and type founder's art, we hope to lead the newspaper public to higher levels than we have ever reached before."

The final page of the post-fire issue also included "To our Outport Friends," a note to subscribers outside of St. John's. It explained that because all the paper's records were lost in the fire, copies of *The Evening Telegram* would only be sent to customers whose names staff remembered. Anybody who had paid for a subscription but failed to receive the paper were asked to contact the office and help straighten out the matter. The note also urged people who were in arrears with the publication to pay their bills promptly. "Our expenses at present are very heavy," it read, "and we hope our friends will attend to this [matter]."

The 25th anniversary edition of *The Evening Telegram*. During that period of the paper's history, it was common to run a high percentage of advertising on the front page.

Subscribers and advertisers didn't appear to be deterred by *The Evening Telegram's* fire-forced hiatus. Sixteen months after it relaunched, the paper moved to its new home on Water Street, beside Gregory's Lane (where the operation would stay until the latter part of the 1950s). As he had done since starting the paper, Herder continued upgrading the equipment. In 1895, he purchased a press capable of pumping out 20,000 four-page newspapers an hour. Eleven years later, he bought another press – the sixth since the inaugural edition. He added other machinery in 1908, including a type-setter. Before introducing that machine, all type-setting was done by hand. In 1917,the press was updated yet again.

Herder had set up his publication so that its editor presided over the content and he, as publisher, looked after the business end of things. He was the first St. John's newspaper operator to do so, and that display of integrity, according to archivist Bert Riggs, is said to have played a major factor in the survival and growth of *The Evening Telegram*. Riggs says another distinguishing mark of the paper was that, unlike most publications in that era, Herder initially did not promote an editorial slant that favoured a particular political side. In the decade following its launch, though, the publication threw its weight behind the Liberal party, and it continued this support until after Herder's death, when it adopted a Newfoundland-first attitude.

Still, there is no denying that Herder stuck to his principles throughout his career. He refused to be pressured by decision makers or people of prominence. On one occasion, that integrity and independence landed him in jail. On August 19, 1898, *The Evening Telegram* published a letter questioning the conduct of Supreme Court officials with young women as they travelled the island doing circuit court. When Herder refused to say who authored the letter, after a short trial that generated headlines across North America, he and his editor Parsons – who stayed with the paper until his retirement in 1901 – were found guilty of contempt and sent to prison for thirty days. Once inside, Herder remained principled. He didn't think he was a criminal and

The Royal Newfoundland Regiment at Beaumont Hamel, July 1916.

wouldn't wear prison attire. Instead, he sat in his underwear. He and Parsons were let out nine days into their sentence after a public petition pressured the governor to release them. The incident is considered a turning point for Herder, *The Evening Telegram*, and even the government of the day. The story would also be passed down through the generations of reporters who worked at the paper. "That used to impress the hell out of us," legendary Newfoundland writer and former *Telegram* reporter Ray Guy told *The Independent*.

There were other occasions when Herder's values and character got him into hot water. At least once, it might have been his wife who was most upset. *The Evening Telegram* had published an editorial that didn't go over well with some citizens. A large group of protesters went to Herder's impressive home on Rennie's Mill Road. The publisher started explaining his reasoning to them and grew angrier as he did. In the middle of the melee, the horse and carriage delivery of a St. John's shop arrived at the house with a parcel for Elizabeth Herder. The package was passed through the mob until it reached the aggravated publisher. He fired it into the house, smashing the contents to pieces. Unbeknown to Herder, it was a set of dishes his wife had ordered. Laughter erupted, the crowd calmed down, and then soon broke up.

In 1909, Herder travelled to London to represent Newfoundland at the First Press Conference, a gathering of journalists from throughout the British Empire. He apparently made a big impression at the event. According to a story published in *The Daily News* years later, "many a tribute has since been paid by [Herder's] colleagues of those days to his geniality, his comradeship and his loyalty to his native land the Empire."

While Herder exhibited strong journalistic principles, he also had a strong flare for promotion (as evidenced in that early item suggesting businesses would do well to advertise with the paper). He made ingenious attempts to get people talking about, and buying, the paper. At one point, he advertised that he would give $500 to the family of a person killed carrying a copy of *The Evening Telegram* while travelling in Newfoundland and Canada. No families ever came looking for the money, although it's a sure bet that if people travelled, they took the paper with them.

By all accounts, staff at *The Evening Telegram* also held Herder in high esteem. He supported reporters' stories. He was demanding with all employees but rarely got angry. "He expected every man to do his duty," pressman Walter Churchill said in a 1972 story. "A quiet and very hard-working man, he could be stern when crossed but never bore a grudge and was quick to forgive." Churchill was seventy-one when that article appeared, and after fifty-six years at *The Evening Telegram*, was still working there. He called the paper's founder "the finest gentleman I have ever known." Perhaps one of the most noteworthy members of Herder's staff was a young man named Joseph R. Smallwood. The man who would later lead Newfoundland into Confederation with Canada and become premier worked at the paper from 1919 to 1922 as a part-time reporter and editorial writer. As a politician, he would often be at odds with *The Evening Telegram* and on one occasion, even hit the paper with a lawsuit.

Herder and his wife had seven sons and five daughters, although two of the girls died young. The boys names were Arthur, Hubert, Ralph, Douglas, William, Augustus (Gus) and James. The surviving daughters were Elsie, Jean and Phyllis. Douglas died of typhoid in 1909 at age twenty-one. And when the world went to war in 1914, five Herder boys got involved (James was too young). Arthur, Hubert and Ralph became members of the Newfoundland Regiment, William assisted in training and Gus tried to enlist but was not accepted due to poor eyesight. According to an article in *The Daily News* published years later, the fact that three Herders showed leadership and were members of the regiment was no surprise. "Chips off the old block," the story said, "what was to be expected."

The First World War brought tragedy. July 1, 1916 – the opening day of the Battle of the Somme – would be the most devastating day in Newfoundland's history. At Beaumont Hamel, as part of the Somme offensive, its regiment was nearly decimated. Over seven hundred members were killed, wounded or missing, and just sixty-eight soldiers answered roll call the next day. The Herders were among the hundreds of families directly affected by the losses. Hubert, a lieutenant and one of the first three Newfoundlanders to join the regiment in August 1914, was among the 255 young men killed in the battle. Ralph was one of the almost 400 injured. (Arthur didn't enlist until later in the war.)

At a time when Herder and others at *The Evening Telegram* were reeling from the massive shock and loss, the publication endeavoured to be a community leader and compassionate voice. It took a few days before the extent of the losses were known back in Newfoundland, and on July 7, the paper ran an editorial headlined all in caps: "KILLED IN ACTION." It stated, "At such a time as this, when to sorrow known is added the fear of sorrow yet to come, we can only speak what words of comfort we may. Yet it is to comfort a country, for it is a country that mourns....The comfort we can give, and the comfort we must feel, must be at the same time our pride. Have not these young men given Newfoundland an honoured place, high even on this long roll of great deeds and deathless names?" During that period, *The Evening Telegram* ran the Union Jack on its editorial page masthead as a show of patriotism, a tradition that continues today.

The Great War's toll on the regiment, and the Herders, didn't end there. On April 14, 1917, Ralph, who had also achieved the rank of lieutenant, was wounded again, this time at Monchy-le-Preux, the French town the Newfoundland Regiment had saved from the Germans by enduring massive counter-attacks. Almost eighteen months later, on Dec. 3, 1917, the Herders faced tragedy yet again. Arthur, who had risen to be lieutenant as well, was killed by a sniper's bullet at Cambrai, another French town, where the Newfoundlanders fought alongside British and Canadian troops. (Soon after that battle, because of its tremendous sacrifices during World War I, the regiment was bestowed the title "Royal.") Arthur's death brought the number of children W.J. and Elizabeth had buried to five.

Herder died on Sunday, May 28, 1922, after fifty-nine years of pioneering Newfoundland's newspaper industry, forty-three of them at *The Evening Telegram*. He hadn't been healthy for some time, but refused to slow his pace. He developed pneumonia while on a ship to Bermuda, a vacation he had been convinced to take. He never fully recovered after his return. His heart weakened and he eventually passed on. His paper paid tribute to him the next day on the editorial page, under the headline "The Passing of a Veteran." The article spoke of the respect Herder had throughout his homeland and the British Empire. He was called a friend of the weak and "implacable foe" of the oppressor. "Possessed of an indomitable spirit, no obstacles were deemed insuperable, and he gradually climbed to the apex of his profession, being at the time of his swift demise, the oldest newspaperman in Newfoundland – the doyen of the press." Herder was still listed on the masthead above the article as the paper's proprietor. The tribute concluded by stating, "*The Telegram*, pride of his life, and the culmination of his earthly life, will miss him, but enshrined in the hearts of every member of the staff will be the memory of William James Herder who was a man among men."

It's an indication of the respect Herder was earned that his chief business rival, *The Daily News*, also recognized and honoured him the day after his death. The competitor heaped praise on W.J., saying he was an outstanding man in many ways and calling him the "Nestor of his Craft." It also recognized him as a esteemed employer, helpful competitor and a respected citizen. "Public life held no attractions for him," the tribute stated, "but few wielded greater influence: and it may be said of him that his influence was wielded conscientiously and in accordance with convictions

W.J. Herder's legacy continues six days a week — almost 130 years after he was told a daily newspaper wouldn't work in St. John's.

strongly held....Those who held similar views regarded him as a bulwark of defence, those who thought differently admired his sturdy independence and manifest sincerity."

As signs of respect, on May 30, 1922, the day of Herder's funeral, *The Evening Telegram* did not publish, and the House of Assembly adjourned. It was a well-attended service that attracted many of St. John's most prominent citizens, including Sir Richard Squires, then prime minister of Newfoundland. He was reported as saying that Herder may not have been a legislator, but he was "a tutor of all legislatures for years passed." Herder was buried in the General Protestant Cemetery. An honour guard walked beside the hearse and his family and employees proceeded behind the casket.

Herder's paper had long silenced any of the early daily-doubters. At the time of his passing, the publication was still seeing impressive annual growth. On the editorial page on the day after he died, the paper's circulation statement listed total

William Herder (left) was named publisher of *The Evening Telegram* after W.J. Herder's passing. Stephen Herder (right) was the last member of the family to hold that position. He held it until 1991.

paper sales for 1921 at 2,591,989, an increase of 212,739 from the previous year and a great leap from the 500 of April 3, 1879. *The Evening Telegram* would continue to grow in circulation and importance. At different periods over the years, it has even been considered the official opposition to government.

After recovering from his war wounds, Ralph went to work at *The Evening Telegram*, along with his brothers William, Gus and James. The Evening Telegram Limited was incorporated in 1922, with William as president and Gus as vice-president. Both passed away in 1934, dying young by today's standards (William was fifty and Gus forty-seven). After their mother died the following summer, Ralph became the president and James the general manager. Ralph held the position until he passed away in 1955. James was company president until 1970. On August 1, 1970 – after ninety-one consecutive years of being published by W.J. Herder and his boys – *The Evening Telegram* was purchased by Thomson Newspapers. A member of the Herder family, though, continued running the paper. Hubert, who had been publisher since 1967, remained in the position until 1976. After that another of W.J.'s grandsons, Stephen, who had been a long-time editor at the paper, became publisher. He held the title until 1991, bringing the family's involvement with the paper to 112 years. Interestingly, the first local publisher of *The Evening Telegram* who wasn't a Herder was Miller Ayre, great-great-grandson of Charles Robert Ayre, the man who helped W.J. get the paper back on the street after the Great Fire of 1892. He took over in 1993 and is now publisher emeritus.

Herder loved fishing and was interested in sports in general. His seven sons excelled at hockey and all played for St. John's teams in the early part of the 1900s (the game was only introduced to Newfoundland in 1896, and was played with a ball and canes). Because of the family's puck prowess, in 1935, a few months after William and Gus died, Ralph decided to establish a trophy in memory of his five deceased brothers. He had a picture of a St. John's player named Edward "Key" Kennedy cast in silver and used it as the centre piece for the Herder Memorial Trophy. The prize was first awarded in 1935 to a team from Corner Brook that had defeated the Guards of St. John's 5-2 in a two-game total goal series. Today, the trophy continues to be awarded to Newfoundland and Labrador's top senior hockey team.

The five brothers whom the trophy is named after were nicknamed "The Dirty Herders." In a 1980 article, Stephen Herder suggested they might have gotten the handle because of their mother's response to hearing one of them taunted as a "Dirty Herder." "Her reaction," he wrote, "took the form of striking the offending commentator in the head with her umbrella." Herder also noted that his cousin Hubert did his part to continue the rugged reputation of W.J.'s sons. According to local lore, he said, Hubert got so upset with one fan during a game at Prince's Rink, near Hotel Newfoundland, that he "leaped over the board and, skates and all, chased him all the way to King's Bridge Road." The incident, however, didn't define Hubert Herder's hockey career. At one time, many considered him the best player in Newfoundland.

Another popular Newfoundland sports endeavour that owes its origin to *The Evening Telegram*, and thus to W.J. Herder, is the annual Tely 10 road race. It was first run in 1922, and has been held every year since, with the exception of World War II years. The first champion was Jack Bell. The guy who finished second, Ron O'Toole, was apparently disappointed that a horse and wagon came between him and the victor during the race. O'Toole went on to win the next three years. The Tely 10 now attracts more than 2,000 competitors.

Herder made a lasting contribution to Newfoundland and the practice of journalism. In 2005, he was chosen as one of the top ten Newfoundlanders and Labradorians of all time by a panel assembled by *The Independent* newspaper. His business sense and accomplishments have also been recognized. He was inducted into the Newfoundland and Labrador Business Hall of Fame on May 13, 2003. His grandson, Jim Herder, accepted the award, stating, "I'm sure when my grandfather started *The Evening Telegram* 124 years ago, he never envisioned that he would one day be honoured and remembered by the people of St. John's. But I'm sure he would be proud. He was a great entrepreneur, and he has been described to me as hard-working, loyal, persistent and tough." A fitting description of a man who left a legacy through determination and by ignoring those who doubted him.

ZITA COBB

SIX-YEAR-OLD Zita Cobb walked out of the sanatorium in Corner Brook ready to conquer the world. She had been in "The San" – as people called the medical facility – battling tuberculosis for a year. It was a long time for a young girl to be 300 miles away from her family on Fogo Island on Newfoundland's northeast coast. She had gone there feeling scared and abandoned, but after fighting the infectious lung disease and realizing a new determination and resilience, she was raring to go upon her release. As an adult, she would look back on her bout with TB as a mercy. "It gave me the confidence that, 'I can do this. I can be on my own at six,' and if you can survive being in a san with dozens and dozens of misbehaved kids, on a ward, practically unsupervised, you can do anything. That just gave me the confidence that I could do whatever I wanted." Once out of the sanatorium, young Zita, for the time being, would have to confine

Photos courtesy of Zita Cobb

Joe Batt's in the winter. Zita relished in her simple and unsupervised childhood there.

her quest to the rocks and hills behind her parents house by the water in the fishing community of Joe Batt's Arm, also known as "Joe Batt's."

Kids organized their own fun in Joe Batt's Arm during the 1960s. They were free agents. After leaving home in the morning, they were at large and able to walk the landwash or catch tom cods or be on the hills setting fires and doing stuff they shouldn't have been doing. There were no adult-organized activities such as Brownies, hockey or soccer, just roving bands of kids who supervised themselves and ran their own activities. They walked everywhere, as there were no rides to be had. They settled their own disputes and shared in their own victories. "Kids had their own little world, and it wasn't the meddling world that kids have now, where their parents were controlling their every move," Zita says. "There was a lot of space in time and geography for your identity to form in a healthy way without your every thought being controlled by an adult." When they were running free, Zita and her friends called it being "on the bon." Despite the lack of grown-up supervision, she didn't get herself into much trouble. The only time she would draw adult ire is when she came home wet and her mother suspected that she had been in the water. Her mom's mother and sister had drowned off nearby Duck Island, so the thought of her children playing around the harbour or in the streams near Joe Batt's Arm made her nervous. "Her great fear in life was that one of us was going to drown so we weren't allowed to go in the water," Zita says.

Mary Zita Cobb was the second youngest of the seven Cobb kids and she was the only girl. The eldest child had been born fifteen years before she was. He had moved out by the time Zita was born, and in her younger years, she always thought her oldest brother was a cousin. Growing up, and enduring, in an environment with so many men was a lesson in itself, and would serve her well when she was outnumbered by men in the business world. "I learned not to be pushed around," she says with a laugh.

Zita's father was an inshore fisherman, who caught and salted cod during the summer and hunted seals in the spring. Her mother raised the kids, cleaned house, and "made fish," which means she dried it. "That was a summer's work," Zita says. "She would take care of the drying as he was doing the catching and the salting, and that was a family enterprise. He would sell it to the merchant." For much of Zita's childhood, the Cobb home never had electricity or running water. The children would do homework by the glow of a kerosene lamp, and everyone chipped in fetching water from a stream near the house. The family grew its own vegetables in a garden on back of their home. They didn't know what it was like to own a vehicle. "Dad never had a license. He never had a car," Zita says.

During her seminal years, Zita formed not only an identity, but also a life plan: By the time she turned forty, she would be finished doing what other people wanted her to do, and would instead be involved in things of her choosing. This line of thinking – precocious for her years – grew out of observing her father and the other fishermen in the close-knit community. She watched them live and work with their economic fate in the hands of others – namely Fogo Island's fish merchants. The buyers would purchase the cod and seal pelts, and the fishermen had little power over how much they got paid; neither did they fully understand what happened to the fish and pelts they had worked so hard to catch. "That's why Dad raised us to change the way we live so that we always had options," Zita says.

She and her father were very close. She says they bonded through arguing about nearly everything, from religion to weather. "He was the kind of guy, you'd say it was a really hot day and he would say it's not that hot," she laughs, before going on to credit her dad with making her a good negotiator. For Zita, the helplessness and frustration of her father's situation really sunk in when the federal government decided that all fisherman had to fill out a tax return. He couldn't read or write, so she did his taxes and discovered that his reward for a year of hard work and life-threatening risks was a meagre $800. Her goal was to not find herself in that place: she wanted to be on the other side of the equation. Mr. Cobb didn't want his daughter to be in the same situation either. "He used to say to me, 'Don't get married and never be beholden to a man,'" Zita recalls. "In other words, always be economically independent. I think that applies to a person, whether a man or a woman, and it applies to a community."

Despite the simple, yet special, wonder of growing up on Fogo Island, by the time she reached seventeen Zita was like many young people who live in rural communities. "I had to get out of here," she says. "Absolutely." She left to attend Carleton University in Ottawa where she studied business. Her parents and Tony, the baby of the family who was two years younger than Zita, also left Joe Batt's Arm around the same time. They moved to Toronto, where Zita's older brothers were living. "There was an air of finality about the way my dad nailed up the gate the morning we left," she wrote in a column for *The Pilot*, a community newspaper that includes Fogo Island in its coverage area. "None of us thought we would be coming back."

After finishing her undergraduate degree, she and a friend bought a "really used" Ontario Hydro van and Zita started fulfilling her goal of exploring the globe. "I was very passionate after I left Fogo Island about travelling," she says. "I really, really wanted to see the world, and that takes time and it takes money.

Fogo Island and its spring ice pans are far removed from corporate boardrooms across North America and around the world.

It actually takes more time than it takes money, and I did appreciate from a very early age that, really, the only currency you have is time and you can use the time you have to turn it into money, but once the time is gone it's all over." They trekked around North America, motoring north to Alaska, throughout the States and Canada, and south to Mexico. Six months into the journey, they ran out of money in Calgary, which Zita recalls as being a good place to be in 1979 with no cash. Anyone with a warm body, she says, could land a job there at that time. She and her friend found work in the oil patch and Zita started down the road to the success she had promised herself as kid.

She worked in accounts with Texaco and Shell. One day early in her second year with Shell, she looked around her workplace and realized she was in the cubicle world. "I remember thinking, 'Wow, if I stay here for ten or fifteen years, maybe I could have that office or that office or maybe even that office.' And then I realized I don't want any of these offices. I don't want this kind of a career. This is not enough to live for. I can't spend my life under fluorescent lights."

Zita moved to a much smaller and much more dynamic company owned by an American firm called Arctec and SNC (which has since evolved into the global engineering and construction conglomerate, SNC-Lavalin). She was still in finance but found herself responsible for all sorts of things, including human resources and purchasing. And unlike those earlier jobs with big oil, the atmosphere was more team-like: a group was trying to grow a small firm into a big one. An added bonus was that the job involved an immense amount of travel, which helped satiate Zita's hunger for exploration. She became the person responsible for consolidating the company's offices acquisitions under one financial roof. She jetted to offices across the continent and learned a lot, especially about the differences between the Canadian and American banking systems. In her home and native land, she discovered, the banks set the rules, which was vastly different from the US, where people interviewed the banks to determine which one they would use.

It was around this time, after she had returned to Fogo Island for a couple of visits, that she started to feel stirred by the place she called home. She began regular trips back and the place grew on her more and more. She and her brothers rebuilt their parents' home and their father's stage. She describes the draw of Joe Batt's Arm by alluding to a quote from T.S. Elliott's *Four Quartets* – *"We shall not cease from exploration/ And the end of all our exploring/ Will be to arrive where we started / And know the place for the first time."* "I rediscovered that Fogo Island is a powerful source of culture, life and inspiration," Zita says. "It is a place that connects people deeply – to each other, to the people who have come before, and to the special physical world it inhabits."

By now residing in Ottawa, Zita stayed with the company until 1988. By then, the Arctec portion of the company had been sold to Fleet Aerospace. Zita was tired. She felt as if she didn't have much more to give the firm, and conversely, that the business didn't have a lot more to offer her in terms of experience. "I had pretty much done it all. It had become a maintenance role and it was a steady state," she says. "That company is still around

Zita and her brothers rebuilt the stage in Joe Batt's Arm that their father used as a fisherman.

today and it still operates in a steady state and it's still a successful Canadian company." Zita didn't know exactly what she wanted to do. She decided to spend some time travelling and took a year-long leave of absence (although her boss knew it was highly unlikely she would return). She headed to the Dark Continent and fell in love with the culture, people, and landscape. "I was bitten by Africa, which never gets out of your system," she says. She returned to Canada after a year there and worked with Arctec for a few more months to help the company prepare for life without her.

In 1989, Zita joined JDS Fitel, a company based near Ottawa in Nepean. The firm was involved in the world of fibre optics and high technology, and Zita had a strong hunch about it. "I knew that telecom would be a great world to be in," she says, "because I was pretty sure the information age was just waiting to be enabled." Zita also appreciated the people who started JDS. They were four guys from Bell-Northern Research who decided to branch out by themselves and make components for fibre optic networks. Among them was the company's eccentric CEO Jozef

Straus. Not only did Zita think they were brilliant, with strong senses for business and technology, she also thought they were decent people, which really mattered to her. "It just seemed like this company was going to do things," says Zita, who accepted the position as the company's chief financial officer.

JDS did do things, though a year after she joined, half the firm was sold to a very large Japanese company. Dealing with a totally different culture, Zita found the new challenges she seemed to crave. She was still unsettled though, and in 1991 with JDS still performing quite well, she took another leave and went to live in Costa Rica for a year. She returned to the company with the intent of staying only a few years. But a new challenge arose when the owners decided to go public on the Toronto Stock Exchange. Intrigued by the direction in which the company was headed, Zita stayed longer than anticipated.

Once listed on the TSE, JDS Fitel continued its rapid growth. Zita explains that it was not a dot-com company, but a firm making real things with real money. It was a profit-making enterprise from the get-go and never had to borrow a penny. Its fortunes grew indescribably greater in the mid-'90s when the upsurge of the Internet resulted in a greater demand for bandwidth. The field of fibre optics went boom, and JDS, with its product that enabled telecommunications firms to boost network capability without putting down new cables, soared to heights no one had ever envisioned. Phone companies everywhere wanted its technology, known as wavelength division multiplexing, or WDM. The challenge in continuing its growth and market dominance, Zita says, was keeping the technology current. "In technology you always feel like you are surfing," she explains. "You are on a wave, and if you don't move properly on that wave, you are going to be absolutely swamped. You would be part of the past really quickly, and so many were. We were pretty good at it." Keeping current involved acquiring a lot of smaller companies who possessed the pieces of technology that fit the JDS puzzle.

In 1996, Zita decided that she would stay with JDS Fitel for another four years. "I felt I would have enough financial resources to not have to sell my time to make a living," she says. "I ended up staying a little bit longer, but I always knew I would leave as soon as I could." The reason she eventually stuck around for a greater period than expected? The company was about to be part of one of the biggest high-tech deals ever. The ascent was just beginning.

JDS was considered a passives company, meaning it made passive optical devices. Straus and the other brains behind the outfit sensed that the world was moving towards more integrated devices, where active and passive technologies were combined in a box. "That was a whole other world," Zita says. "We couldn't see getting there by just buying little companies." Around the same time, the company was eying a different dimension altogether – the NASDAQ stock exchange in the US. To satisfy the need for active technology and make the company carry more weight on one of the world's busiest stock exchanges, JDS merged with Uniphase Corp.

Zita with Jozef Straus, the colourful CEO of JDS Uniphase.

The San Jose-based company was the largest player in the active optics world at that time, and was looking at getting into the passives field. "It was a merger of equals," says Zita.

The deal was reportedly initiated by Straus, who asked Uniphase CEO Kevin Kalkhoven to join him for a hike in the Rockies to talk shop. Cobb was quoted in *Maclean's* as describing the hike as a "classic male bonding experience." It would become a classic corporate bonding experience too. JDS Uniphase Corp. became official in June 1999 and, in the language of pop music charts, the new conglomerate was a hit. In less than a year, at more than $64 billion, JDS Uniphase had a market value equaling the combined worth of Canada's three largest banks. As well, shares of the company peaked at almost $220. JDS's stocks were $28.75 at the time of the corporate marriage with Uniphase, so soaring to almost eight times that value made grateful shareholders grin. It prompted one to walk up to Straus and kiss the CEO on the cheek in a hotel lobby.

Zita's title with JDS Uniphase was senior vice-president of strategy and integration. As she had done with JDS Fitel, she helped the new company grow exponentially as it merged with smaller companies in order to stay on top of its game and stock value. "It was an incredible journey," she says. When Zita started with JDS, she joined a team of ninety people. After the amalgamation with Uniphase, she saw the number of company employees soar to the tens of thousands. Despite the rapid growth of worth and workforce, she wondered about her own growth. She started feeling as if she was headed for the same place she had been in ten years earlier. She didn't expect that she was going to learn a whole lot more, and didn't see herself as critical to the company's future – even though by 2000 she was reported to be the third highest paid female business executive in North America.

In the spring of 2001, Zita took a leave of absence. She left at a time when there was a downturn in the market and the company was experiencing some turbulence. Her colleagues on JDS Uniphase's executive and the stock market analysts were concerned about her leave. "I guess we'll have to see whether this is really temporary," Charles Willihoit of JP Morgan and Co. said in an interview. "She's been a very important part of the team, particularly behind the scenes. We'd be sad to see her go." A while later, Zita retired as one of the wealthiest women in Canada. Her shares in JDS alone were worth hundreds of millions, and that didn't include other investments and savings. "I certainly didn't have to work anymore, financially," she says, "and I just had a lot of things I wanted to do."

Zita never quite fulfilled her childhood dream of not working for someone else by the time she reached forty, but making it happen by the time she was forty-two was pretty darn close.

Zita was a valuable part of the JDS Uniphase team but the draw of the land and sea was too powerful for her to remain in the corporate world.

There was another reason the determined woman wanted to start doing her own thing. She comes from a family of people who die young. Two of her brothers suffered heart attacks and died before their time, and most of her mother's brothers passed away in their forties. "I grew up with a belief that if I make it to fifty, that's really pushing it," Zita says. "I never felt I had time to squander. I still don't." She turned fifty in the summer of 2008 and is trying to do what she can to boost her chances of staying around for as long as possible. She is a heart-healthy eater and an avid runner who is seen trotting down the roads and trails of Fogo Island in all kinds of weather. "When I run, every run, my brothers are with me," she says. "My mother, who died of a massive heart attack, my father who died of a heart attack, I run for them. They are with me when I run."

As for her wealth, Zita says she felt as if she had money when she landed her first job back in Calgary in the late seventies – especially when her annual income was compared to the $800 her father had made for a full year of working the sea. "My first salary

Zita says she used Newfoundland humor to her advantage in her business dealings.

was $14,000 a year and I was quite young...I thought that was a fortune," she says. "I always felt wealthy from the moment I started working, but not wealthy enough to quit."

Being a Newfoundlander, Zita says, played a key role in her climb to the top of the corporate ladder. She thinks people from her home province have an unfair advantage everywhere they go because they are brave and refreshingly direct. "It was easy," she says. "I just found that the kind of personality traits that most of us as Newfoundlanders have, you put them in the business world and they are exactly what the business world needs." Zita feels people felt they could trust her, which really made a huge difference when handling other people's money and while negotiating deals all over the world. In one two-year span, she illustrates, she helped buy forty companies. She says such purchases don't happen with just lawyers and legal agreements. "You make deals on the basis of personal accord and there is something about Newfoundlanders. We're good at that. We're good at that because I think we are real. We're authentic." Relying heavily on natural Newfoundland humour, Zita felt she could say anything to anybody and get away with it. "It's a Newfoundland thing, don't you think?"

The trait was particularly helpful when doing deals in a country like Japan, where she was involved in a lot of high-level meetings throughout her years with JDS and JDS Uniphase. A female business executive, especially one as bold and direct as Zita, was something the company's Japanese associates had not experienced. Japanese women typically stopped working after they got married and rarely made it to the top offices of corporations. Zita's status prompted one Japanese businessman to tell her that, from working with her, they had discovered there were actually three sexes. "I said, 'Really.' And he said, 'Yes. There's women and there's men and there's women in business,' " Zita remembers him saying. " 'We don't quite know what to make of you,' he said. 'You're kind of like a woman, but not really.' It was hardly a society where women had got very far in business. It still isn't great. The best thing to do is kind of mow your own field, which is what I did." Zita says her boss picked up on the uneasiness of his Japanese colleagues and said, "They just don't know what to make of you, so they just have no choice but to respond to you authentically." In all the years she dealt with the Japanese, she never encountered another woman near the helm of a company. It didn't phase her though. "I grew up being the only woman," Zita says. "It was okay. I knew that road."

She admits there were times during her career when she would be in a board room in Tokyo and suddenly realize how far she was from the hills behind her parents' house in Joe Batt's Arm or the landwash in front of it. But it seemed perfectly natural to

> "I just found that the kind of personality traits that most of us as Newfoundlanders have, you put them in the business world and they are exactly what the business world needs."
>
> ZITA COBB

Joe Batt's Arm at night. Zita would sit in boardrooms around the world and realize how far she had travelled from scenes like this.

her. Like her desire to do what she wanted to by forty, she had imagined being involved at an international level in her youth. "I remember," she says, "being on a hill behind our house watching airplanes go over, and you see their contrails, thinking, 'One day I'll be on board those flights.' "

And during those high-level business meetings, Zita often relied on part of her upbringing to help make the right decisions. She used the philosophy her father acquired through his life and passed down to her. She says you can't make business deals without tripping over serious ethical questions from time to time, forcing you to ask yourself, "Wait, can I live with this?" Whenever that happened, Zita says she would always think back to her father and use him as a reference point. She would ask herself, "What would Dad do? What would he say about that?" Still, Zita says she was extremely competitive in the business world. When going after a company that was really needed, she says she was pretty determined and focused on getting it. "And I understood that not everybody is going to make it, and not everybody should make it," she says. "And I was focused on the fact that we just need to make sure that ours does [make it]."

Zita's mom passed away in 1981 and her dad died in 1988. Both were brought home from Toronto to Fogo Island to be buried. They never had a chance to see the impressive financial status their daughter would attain. Surely it would be hard for a couple who never had running water, electricity, or a car while raising their family to fathom that their little girl had become one of the wealthiest women in Canada. If he were alive, despite her fortune and the respect she commanded in the boardrooms of places like Japan, Zita figures her father would still be full of suggestions about what she should and shouldn't be doing. "I often hear his voice saying, 'You going to let that go on that way?'"

He would undoubtedly be proud and supportive of what she has done since her official retirement. When she said good-bye to JDS Uniphase, one of Zita's dreams was to become a social entrepreneur and help remote communities such as the ones she loved in Africa or the places that were dear to her on a little island off the northeast coast of Newfoundland. So, besides sailing around the world – which she did – Zita started a registered Canadian charity. It got involved in radio education projects in rural parts of Africa as well as development projects in her native Newfoundland and Labrador, particularly the Fogo Island-Change Islands area. That area and its way of life are dear to her. She knows the past thirty or forty years haven't been kind to Fogo Island, or rural places in general. She wants to preserve it and secure the future. Although she maintains a condo at one of Ottawa's most prestigious addresses, she spends most of her time on Fogo Island. "I could have gone anywhere," Zita says. "I spend all winter here. I think people get that you didn't need to do that. But I want to do that. I think this is a special place to be."

Her non-profit organization was originally called the Frangipani Foundation. It got its name from a tropical tree that has beautiful blossoms and a sap that is used in parts of Africa to heal wounds. The organization has since evolved into the

The way of life on Fogo Island and Change Islands remains dear to Zita.

Shorefast Foundation, which fittingly gets its name from a line that secures a cod trap to the shore. The organization currently uses business strategies to strengthen the economy of Fogo Island and Change Islands. It's social entrepreneurship in action. Shorefast wants to help people start businesses and make their own way. It also wants to carry out its own projects in order to help the islands prosper. "I really believe that you can combine business with social ends," Zita says. "And I believe that social entrepreneurship will provide part of the answer for places like Fogo Island to find an economic path that is sustainable. And not just sustainable economically, but one that helps them sustain community and heritage and involve the young people that we have to have or we'll all be lost." The intent is to find ways to take the things the people of the islands have always done well and connect the products of those activities with outside markets. "Imagine then," Zita says, "that you have an economy that is based on who you are. That is absolutely how you preserve

She owns a punt and believes preserving Fogo Island's boat-building heritage is important.

culture." The key, she suggests, is linking to markets directly, so people don't have to go through a merchant or broker and can control their destiny.

A lot of Shorefast's work thus far has centered on preserving and capitalizing on the wooden boat heritage of Fogo Island and Change Islands. It has collected wooden boats, initiated traditional boat-building projects and started a one-of-a-kind boat-building program with students and staff at Fogo Island Central Academy. It's also facilitated a new event, The Great Fogo Island Punt Race, which sees pairs of rowers race punts from Fogo Island to Change Islands and back. The distance is 10.5 miles and the course is challenging, especially if Mother Nature is in a foul mood (it is the north side of Newfoundland after all). "The idea here is twofold," says David Carlson, who was on the organizing committee of the first regatta in 2007. "One is to get people out rowing again and the other is to preserve and promote our wooden boat-building heritage." The event has so far been a resounding success. It doubled in participants in its second year, with twenty-one punts and forty-two racers registering.

Shorefast is also behind the start-up of the World's End Theatre Company, which in 2008 began its efforts to stage professional theatre reflecting life on Fogo Island and Change Island. The troupe's first summer saw it produce an original play called *Fighting Fire with Snow*. It's no surprise that Shorefast is using artistic endeavours as part of its efforts on the islands. Zita is passionate about the power of arts as an economic and social engine, and she has some impressive experience and connections in the world of the arts. In 2007, for example, she was a member of the Penelope Circle, a group of high-profile Canadian women who helped mount *The Penelopiad*. Staged at the National Arts Centre in Ottawa, it was a collaboration between legendary Canadian writer Margaret Atwood and the Royal Shakespeare Company. And in early 2008, Zita was appointed a director of the National Arts Centre Foundation. "My belief is that our society hasn't quite figured out how to give arts and artists their due," she says. "I think they should be at the table for discussions on a variety of things. I really see the interdependencies of things, and business is not separate from the arts. It really needs to come together." She insists the arts will play a role in what Shorefast does on the islands.

> "So far...all I've done is I've been a very good technician in other people's games."
>
> ZITA COBB

Along with boat-building and theatre, traditional activities on which Shorefast hopes to help people capitalize include things such as berrypicking, carpentry, cooking, farming, fishing, mat-hooking, quilt making, singing and storytelling. "Through them and by mastering teamwork and finding new connections to marketplaces," Zita wrote in a column published in *The Pilot*, "we can sustain our community and secure our future."

Zita spends most of her time back on Fogo Island, working alongside childhood friends like Pete and Margaret Decker.

In February 2008, Zita's efforts on Fogo Island received attention across Newfoundland and Labrador when the popular CBC-TV program *Land and Sea* aired an episode about her rags to riches story. Her journey and vision for Fogo Island's future appeared to leave an impression on Fred Greening, the show's producer. "She is prepared to put her money where her mouth is," he told *The Pilot* before "Zita of Fogo" aired. "She sees the island as a culturally diverse place with each community bringing its own identity, which should be protected, but [she also] sees the island as but one economic community, and a small one at that." Fittingly, during the show, Zita tells Greening that every rock on Fogo Island matters to her.

Zita says some people, including decision-makers, have a hard time understanding exactly what a social entrepreneur is, as well as some of the things she is trying to do. People ask if she is in the not-for-profit or for-profit world. Her reply is yes. "It's very confusing," she laughs. But to Zita, it's quite clear. She hopes it's a remedy for the land she loves. And despite her immense financial wealth, she believes it's succeeding at being a social entrepreneur that will make her truly prosperous. "So far...all I've done is I've been a very good technician in other people's games," Zita says. "What I want to do is to actually find the means, whether my own personal resources – I don't just mean financial resources – to do my part to make the world a better place."

Zita says she could spend winters anywhere in the world but chooses Fogo Island.

STEVE BARTLETT

ACKNOWLEDGEMENTS

Numerous people deserve my appreciation and thanks. My wife, Melanie, patiently endured countless hours of having to repeat herself because I was in a computer trance. Donna Francis at Creative Book Publishing survived listening to my excuses for not getting this done faster. Donna's staff — Janine Lilly, Joanne Snook-Hann, and Todd Manning — also have my gratitude. They made me look good. And speaking of people who did that, my editor, Ed Kavanagh, made this read a lot better than it was written. Thanks also to Daphne Bartlett, Nathan Bartlett, Alan Bock, Dan Helmbold and Jacqui Walsh. And of course, my special thanks go out to the people who made this book possible by giving interviews, sharing information and providing photos: Jim Bennett, Lisa Bennett, Mildred Bennett, Trevor Bennett, Alan Cobb, Tony Cobb, Zita Cobb, Alex Faulkner, Shawn Faulkner, James Herder, Greg Malone, and Sara Sexton. Surely I forgot someone, and if that happens to be you, I apologize. It wasn't intentional.

BIBLIOGRAPHY

"A Life of Service." Community Memories. Virtual Museum of Canada
     8 Mar. 2008
     <www.virtualmuseum.ca/pm.php?id=exhibit_home&fl=0&lg=English
     &ex=00000240&pg=1>

"AIDS centre keeps Sexton's memory alive." *CBC News*
     [St. John's] 16 Sept. 2006. 8 Sept. 2008
     <http://www.cbc.ca/canada/newfoundlandlabrador/story/2006/09/15/se
     xton-centre.html>

"Alex Faulkner's hockey statistics profile at hockeyDB.com."
     hockeyDB.com
          11 July 2008
     <http://www.hockeydb.com/ihib/stats/pdisplay.php?pid=1625>

"A tradition of Excellence." *The Evening Telegram*
     [St. John's] 26 April 2003: B14

Baird, Moira. "Nfld. Company lists on New York Stock Exchange."
     The Western Star
     [Corner Brook] 12 Oct. 2002: A16

Baird, Moira. "Dobbin's death a loss for Newfoundland." *The Telegram*
     [St. John's] 8 Oct. 2006:A1

Baird, Moira. "Mediocre politicians harming province: Dobbin."
     The Telegram
     [St. John's] 27 Feb. 2003:A1

Bierworth, Sandy. "Telegram founder among Hall of Fame inductees."
     The Telegram
     [St. John's] 14 May 2003: A1

"CHC buying Netherlands' Schreiner Aviation for $129 million."
     CBC News
     [St. John's] 1 Dec. 2003. 21 Dec. 2006
     <http:www.cbc.ca/money/story/2003/12/01/chc_031201.html.>

Canadian Press. "CHC now largest chopper leaser." *The Evening News* [New Glasgow] 25 June 1999: A6

Canadian Press. "In his father's footsteps." *The Telegram* [St. John's] 11 Oct. 2006: D1

Cobb, Zita. "Finding new connections." *The Pilot* [Lewisporte] 9 July 2008: B3

"Convocation address by Dr. Craig Dobbin." President's Report/Honour Roll 1999-2000/Craig Dobbin. Memorial University of Newfoundland.
8 Jan. 2007 <http://mun.ca/president/99-00report/honor/honorary_dobbin.htm/>

"Convocation address by Dr. Greg Malone." President's Report/Honour Roll 1999-2000/Greg Malone. Memorial University of Newfoundland.
24 Aug. 2008 <http://mun.ca/president/99-00report/honor/honorary_malone.html#address>

"Dobbin has his finger on political pulse." *The Telegram* [St. John's] 1 Mar. 2003: A10

Harrington, Michael. "A Newspaper's Centennial." *The Atlantic Advocate* [Fredericton] May 1979: 10

"Helicopter magnate Dobbin hailed as a 'patriot,visionary.' " *CBC News* [St. John's] 8 Oct. 2006. 21 Dec. 2006 <http://www.cbc.ca/news/story/2006/10/08/dobbin-obit.html>

Jander, Mary. "JDSU deepens reorg." *Light Reading*. 24 April 2001.
1 Sept. 2008 <http://www.lightreading.com/document.asp?doc_id=4848>

Laver, Ross. "JDS Uniphase Corporation." *Maclean's*. 27 Mar. 2000.
    1 Sept. 2008
<http://www.thecanadianencyclopedia.com/index.cfmPgNm=TCE&Par
ams=M1ARTM0012155>

"Local and other items." *The Evening Telegram*
    [St. John's] 9 April, 1879: 4

Martin, Cabot. "He galvanized the room." *The Independent*
    [St. John's] 13 Oct. 2006: A13

McLeod, Lori. "To be forever young." *Canada.com*. 9 Dec. 2006.
    27 Dec. 2006
<http://www.canada.com/topics/finance/story.html?id=46c94e50- bde-
4671-8950-5ec245d3d385&k=71224>

Mullowney, Tara. "Built international business empire, Craig Dobbin
laid to rest." *The Western Star*
    [Corner Brook] 10 Oct. 2006: A8

Newman, Peter C. "October 2001 – Igniting the entrepreneurial
spark." Corporate Responsibility Publications, RBC Financial Group.
    10 Jan. 2007
<http://www.rbc.com/community/letter/october2001.html>

Pitts, Gordon. "The Codfathers: Lessons from the Atlantic business
elite." Toronto:
    Key Porter Books Limited, 2005.

Porter, Stephanie. "Basically, he's still around," *The Independent*
    [St. John's] 4 Sept. 2005: A2

Riggs, Bert. "The man behind *The Telegram*." *The Telegram*
    [St. John's] 6 Oct. 1998:B2

Short, Robin. "Fog Devils will call Mile One home for 5 years."
The Western Star
    [Corner Brook] 4 Mar. 2005: A14

Stokes Sullivan, Deana. "Centre receives generous support from
Dobbins." *The Western Star*
[Corner Brook] 14 Dec. 2005: A4

"To Business Men." *The Evening Telegram*
[St. John's] 8 April, 1879: 4

"The Passing of a Veteran." *The Evening Telegram*
[St. John's] 29 May, 1922: 4

"The Telegram's History," *The Telegram*
11 Oct. 2008,
<http://www.thetelegram.com/index.cfm?pid=1193>

"The Telegram's Herder Memorial Hockey Championship Series
History," *The Telegram*
11 Oct. 2008,
<http://www.thetelegram.com/index.cfm?pid=2506>

"Vale." *The Evening Telegram*
[St. John's] 31 May, 1922: 4

Wells, Karen. "Off to the races." *The Telegram*
[St. John's] 4 Aug. 2007: F1

Wells, Karen. "Zita of Fogo Island: Land and Sea takes a look at her
story." *The Pilot*
[Lewisporte] 13 Feb. 2008:B2

Weir, Gail. "The Papers of CODCO." Memorial University Libraries
30 Aug. 2008
<http.library.mun.ca/qeii/cns.archives/codco.php>

"W.J. Herder: His work lives on." *The Evening Telegram*
[St. John's] 28 May 1972:A 4